# Fire in the Belly

# Fire in the Belly

Sumer Sethi, MD

PRABHAT
PRAKASHAN

*Published by*
**PRABHAT PRAKASHAN PVT. LTD.**
4/19 Asaf Ali Road,
New Delhi-110 002 (INDIA)
e-mail: prabhatbooks@gmail.com

ISBN 978-93-86231-68-0
**FIRE IN THE BELLY**
*by* Sumer Sethi, MD

*Edition*
2025

*Paperback Price*
₹ 500.00 (Rupees Five Hundred only)



*Printed at*
Narula Printers, Delhi

*To All My Students*

# Author's Note

My journey began many years ago as a bright student in an average school. It was a journey plagued with self-doubts and relentless desire to succeed. I did my schooling from an ordinary school and I had no example of alumni who had made it to medical school or had done 'that' well in life. Being from a family, with not so strong background. I had no example to quote of a business or entrepreneurship from family. There were always people around studying in better schools, having the privileges of family legacies to go ahead.

Despite enormous self-doubts, my desire to excel was always stronger than them. I gave my AIPMT and got a single digit rank in it leaving behind lakhs of my colleagues, fellow mates. As the old adage goes: 'HISTORY DID REPEAT ITSELF' and by God's grace I again got single digit rank in All India PG medical entrance leaving behind not students but doctors this time. I did my postgraduation in Radiology which was, is and will be the subject close to my heart.

This was the time when the entrepreneurship bug bit me and I started my own medical education enterprise called 'DAMS', which today has a country-wide presence. I have mentored lakhs of doctors and Dentists guiding them preparing them for various exams since 1999. My love for technology and academic excellence helped me establish video conference-based classroom for doctors, far away and near reaching every nook and corner of country and tablet-based courses being first of its kind. I started tele-medicine with TeleRad Providers with a goal to provide high-quality radiological education to the tier II and III cities. I don't see this as the end of journey but rather an another bend. I still don't say I am successful. I am just "one of you" with some ideas which helped me tread the path of success in my, which I have been sharing with young medical students over scores of mentoring sessions both in form of workshops and individual discussion forums. This book is a collection of those "discussions" which I ended up writing whenever, I could get hold of a phone laptop or simple pen and paper so as to say, in this fast-paced life. For me it was a sigh of relief when the air hostess announced that "it was safe to use our electronic devices then."

I apologise for the fact the some of the articles may not be coherent or in sequence with the flow of the book for in general because that is the way life is. Each individual has a different viewpoint, different set of needs and these articles are based on those interactions.

There are several traits and ideas which help you reach where you want to be, but what I have learnt it all begins with intense.

Desire to do well.

Desire to excel and shine.

Desire to make a difference.

Desire to touch lives.

For the Proverbial, " Fire in the Belly" is the initiator of everything that a man achieves.

# Editor's Note

Well where to start from I don't know. Dr. Sumer heads Delhi Academy of Medical Sciences, DAMS and is among one of the known radiologists of country. With many publications in worldwide famous journals of the country...and chief executive officer of Telerad Providers he chooses to stay modest about his achievements. With a keen interest in writing and through his vision as we will see in the next few pages he proves that he is not only the best radiologist but also a good writer...you give him time which is a scarcity for him and a pen and he will have something penned down... Dr. Sumer doesn't like to be left behind anyone in this highly competitive world and so keeps himself updated with latest technology out there in the market. Passionate for teaching he would do his best efforts to drill into your mind and would stay there till you are happy. Ever helping on the toes he would be and will be available round the corner. You just need to approach him... Facebook. Twitter everywhere anywhere he is going to be there. It is inspiring to learn from the mentor, who is a pioneer in medical tele-education and tele-medicine vertical in India.

Blessed with a four-year-old son who seems to be following his father's steps...and his better half Dr. Deepti Sethi he seems to have balanced his life just too well and hasn't ever stopped to look behind with an always rising attitude...compassionate as a teacher honest and humble father, ever – caring husband and above all the best radiologist and doctor he is one-in-all...reading about him just won't be enough you need to meet him to get the precious words of wisdom and once you have his hand over your head. There is no look back for you... you have already kept your foot on the stair of success you have started climbing. Backed by Dr. Deepti he has not only produced "one of the kind" medical education network in India but also produced some of the finest doctors around. Yes we come from DAMS.

Yes we have been blessed by Dr. Sumer.

Yes we can cross any hurdle.

Yes we are best for we have the best guru by our side.

That is all I can say.

**—Dr. Vivek Ahuja**
(2015 DAMS)

# Acknowledgements

My Parents Subhash Chander Sethi and Mrs. Karuna Sethi for being a constant source of encouragement and inspiration throughout.

My wife Deepti Sethi for her support and patience without which this project would never have been possible. My Son Krish for bearing with me in the manuscript preparation. Your support is my backbone.

Dr. Sidharth Kumar Sethi, Dr. Shilpa Singla, Sumati, Mr. Deepak Bahl, Mrs. Geeta Bahl and Dr. Jagdish Arora for the wishes and support. Dr. Rajiv Bhagi for all his support always.

Ms. Sunita Sharma for helping to collect my random articles from my facebook profiles. Mr Aayush Sharma for his immense contribution in getting everything organized meticulously and always believing in the possibility of this book.

Special mention to Ms. Shashi Gupta for the illustrations and book cover. Without her creativity the book wouldn't have got the final shape that it has now.

Thank you Dr. Vivek Ahuja (Proud DAMS Student 2015 Batch) for helping to edit the material.

# Contents

*Author's Note* 7
*Editor's Note* 9
*Acknowledgements* 11

**FIRE IN THE BELLY**

1. Fire in the Belly 21
2. Prisoner of Fear 23
3. Insight 24
4. Did You Lose Your 'Mojo' on the Way? 25
5. When Dreams Don't Let You Sleep 26
6. Let Them Rule You Out 27
7. Recreating Beginner's Luck 28
8. Bird of Success 31
9. Drive 32
10. Don't Ask Me to Dream Logically 33
11. Smell of Victory 34
12. Fake Contentment 35
13. No Regrets 36
14. Cut the Ropes 38
15. Retirement at 40: Myth or Reality 39
16. Fears and Dreams 40
17. Was this it? 41

18. Madness 42
19. Consistency is the Key 43

## LEADERSHIP

20. Sculpturing and Leadership 47
21. Nitpicking Kills the Team 48
22. Google's New CEO: One More for the 'Argumentative' Ones 49
23. Role You Play 51
24. Friction 52
25. Seeing from Others' Side Their Perspective 53
26. The Perfect Team with Perfect People: Myth or Reality 54
27. Secret to Success: Put Others First 56
28. Different 'Worlds' 57
29. People Change 58
30. Team Building and 'Temple Run' 60

## HANDLING FAILURE

31. Take Help, Seek Other's Perspective 63
32. Hanging On 64
33. The Moment When You Almost Gave it Up 65
34. Invisible Walls 66
35. Courage 68
36. Quitters 69
37. The Other Side of the Story 70
38. Winners Tell a 'Modified' Story 71
39. What not to Do When You are Feeling Low 72
40. One Day a Miracle will Occur 74
41. Best Teacher in Life – Failure 75
42. Experience 76
43. The Ones Who Lag Behind 77

## WINNER'S SECRET


44. Success has a Price to be Paid 81
45. When You Doubt Your Power, You Give Power to Your Doubt 82
46. Rhythm and Momentum: Winner's Secret Tools 84
47. Power of 'The Moment' 86
48. Passionate Yet Detached 87
49. Meaning of Success 88
50. Insecurity, Expectations and Freedom 90
51. 'Mediocrity' is Easy 91
52. Despite All the 'Odds' 92
53. Road Less Travelled 93
54. Let's Learn to Play to Win in Three Quick Simple Steps 95
55. The Question is not 'How' but 'Why' 96
56. Gap Between 'Saying' and 'Doing' 97
57. Killer Instinct 99
58. Secret Behind 'Compromise' 101
59. Ability to 'Shut Off' Stress 102
60. Thought to Action – Lag Time 104
61. Only Change is Permanent 105


## DECISION MAKING


62. Choices You Make 109
63. To Wait for the Dream Bus or Board the One that is Right There in Front of You 111
64. Taking the 'Call' 113


## TIME MANAGEMENT


65. Manage Your Time Better: Identify the Spurts 117
66. Value Your Own Time 119

67. Paradox of "Too much to Do, too Little Time" 120
68. Sand in Your Hand 122

## THINKING OUT OF THE BOX

69. Something Should be Done, At Least They are Doing Something 125
70. Sceptic, with a Bit of Faith 127
71. Knowledge on the Edge 128
72. Winds of Change 129
73. Look Beyond Self-Imposed Boundaries 130
74. Ultrasound in the Shopping Centre 131
75. Lateral Thinking 133
76. Learn to Unlearn 134
77. Planning Versus Intuitiveness 135
78. Intellectual Cowardice 137
79. Taj Mahal Seekers 139
80. Fringe Vision 141
81. Let's not Kill the Innovation and Scepticism 143
82. Flexibility-Identify the 'Nudges' 145
83. Innovation: The How and Why of It 146
84. Extrapolation 147
85. Limited by Thought 149
86. Little Bit of Madness 150
87. Afraid to Think Different, Are You? 151

## WORK AND LIFE

88. Time Flies 155
89. Timeless Moments 156
90. Real Stories have No Conclusions 157
91. What If? 158
92. Keeping Pace with Life 159

93. Postponing Life 160
94. Chase 161
95. Ephemeral Kingdom 162
96. Destiny 163
97. Wings of Freedom 164
98. Are We Becoming a 'Jerkistan' 167
99. Virtual Relationships 169
100. Stuck in the City of Dreams 170
101. Age Thermostat 171
102. Put ***Your Feet*** in ***My Shoes***, and See What it is Like 172
103. Mindless Conversations 174

## COMMON SENSE

104. Living Up to a Mirage of Self-Image 177
105. Freedom from Being Judged 178
106. Beware of Chauffeur Knowledge in Medical Education 179
107. Being Yourself 181
108. Vision, Common Sense and Criticism 182
109. 'You are Right But...' 183
110. Art of Listening 184
111. How Many Teachers do You Remember in Life? 186
112. Bird Eye's View to Your Rescue 188
113. "What if it's All a Lie?" 189
114. Imitation Without Passion 190
115. To Know that "I Don't Know" is the Key 191
116. Things You cannot Control 192
117. Imperfections 193
118. Prejudice 194
119. Aim for Progress not Perfection 195
120. Far Away World 196

## GRATITUDE

121. World Without You 199
122. Do You Have Some Free 'Space'? 200
123. Sense of Entitlement 202
124. Circle of Good 203
125. Be Humble, Be Yourself 204
126. Gratitude 205

## CREATIVITY

127. The Coffee House 209
128. Ideas are Parasites 211
129. Will Crowd Sourcing One Day Solve the Mystery of Life? 212
130. 'I am Bored' Leads to Creativity 213
131. Circle of Thought 214
132. Wheels and Wings (Fiction) 215

## ENTREPRENEURSHIP

133. The Test of 'Time' 219
134. Organized Chaos 221
135. King Midas and the Story of Entrepreneurship 222
136. Find Your True Passion 223
137. People Never Forget How You Made Them Feel 224
138. Touching Lives 225
139. Gambler's Spirit 226
140. Leap of Faith 227
141. Nokia Story: World is Changing Faster than You can Imagine 229
142. Doctors and Entrepreneurship 231

# FIRE IN THE BELLY

# Fire in the Belly

Many times I meet people who pose questions like "Why should one make so much effort to do their work when even after doing all this, all you eat is normal food?" "Do I actually have a purpose for my efforts?" When I introspect and think, I realize it is the '**fire in my belly**', the desire to win which pushes me to put that extra effort into what I do and go the extra mile.

Most people who fail to achieve their goals are the people who don't have the desire to win, which may be because of two reasons – either they chose the wrong goal or they don't have "fire in their belly". These are the people who question why do athletes run, jump and push themselves to the limits, why did Sachin Tendulkar play the game for so long, even after records and money stopped making a difference.

Reason is in the feeling you get at the moment of glory which the winners get addicted to. It is spurt of adrenaline surge, exhilaration, and moment of thrill which an athlete feels while crossing the line, similar to 'Formula 1' racer who sees the chequered flag. There is always a risk involved in stretching yourselves beyond your limits but desire to win outweighs all the risks and doubts. It is not true that winners don't doubt their capacities and abilities, but they win despite all the odds, all the doubts. Everybody's life is like a sea-saw where there are phases when we feel low and phases when we want to touch the stars. You have to find something that fires your imagination, and then go all out for your moment of glory. There are always many reasons not to play but there is only reason to play, the desire to win. You can remain static and safe forever theoretically speaking, but as Napoleon said, "a moment of glory is worth more than a lifetime of obscurity."

From one of the most popular watched TV shows: You know who cries hardest in the Miss America Pageant?

The winner. Because she knows she can't win again, and winners always want to win more.

□

## Prisoner of Fear

Most dreaded day in his life was about to arrive. He kept thinking of the consequences. He wished this day would go away. He could not sleep with anxiety. This was his greatest fear. He had tried his level best to avoid it. His instinct had always been that of avoidance rather than facing the music. Each day he was suffered, he wanted to somehow avoid that day.

As the day approached, he could feel his breath getting heavier. He was feeling suffocated/choked. He could neither eat nor sleep. He spent time and effort in finding place to hide. He wanted to be invisible.

*But then the 'D' day came. Everything that had to go wrong did go wrong. He suffered. Yes, he did a lot.*

But also felt liberated. He was no longer the prisoner of fear.

As is the age old **Murphy's Law "Anything that can go wrong, will go wrong."**

□

# Insight

## Prologue

Deep down he always knew what his next step should be, his intuition was stronger than his doubts. Brief moments of solitude always told him what was the right thing. But was reluctant to trust his instincts. He argued with his own self, sought popular opinion on what he should do. He rationalised the pros and cons of his decisions. He drowned his intuition with arguments and opinions.

Few years down the lane:

He was an old man now. He had lived his life conforming to what he was supposed to do. You could not find a technical flaw in his judgements. He had been successful to say the least.

*But deep down inside the heart he knew "something was missing." Somewhere deep down he knew he had compromised dreams for rationality. That was his final thought. The last regret.*

## Epilogue

We all somehow know what we want to do but we still keep continue to do to the contrary and believe that one day we will do what we dream of if we compromise today.

□

# Did You Lose Your 'Mojo' on the Way?

You always wanted to win. You had the hunger and passion to win. You had nothing to lose. You took your chances and played by instinct. You won! Yes you won significantly.

After winning you rationalise your win. You attribute it to your foresight, calculations and planning in life.

Somehow you are unable to recreate the initial magic. That's so common in life bright students in school somehow don't come out to be that bright in professional life.

Somehow their victory was because of their attitude and faith on 'gut feeling'. They attributed it to less important reasons and became a one-match wonder.

*You need to get your wild spirit back.*

*You need to ask yourself once a while, "did you lose your 'mojo' on the way?"*

□

## When Dreams Don't Let You Sleep

This one is not for the soft hearted. This one is not for the conservatives not even for the lazy ones.

*This one is for 'dreamers'.*

There is so much to do in one's life, that at times I feel like just one life is not enough to fulfil all your hearts desires. I want to get as much as I can out of life, as possible. That's the battle every day, between sleep and doing something productive.

You may call me fidgety, you may call me workaholic, you may feel I am over ambitious, but I don't want to regret things I didn't do.

*As Dr. Abdul Kalam said "The dream is not what you see in sleep, dream is which does not let you sleep".*

□

## Let Them Rule You Out

Yes, they might ostracize you out based on your background, looks, grades and schools. They will tell you: You are not supposed to win. You are not supposed to be the one here. You are just an average kid.

There will be critics. They get uncomfortable with your non-conformist behaviour. They will do everything possible to drag you down.

*They will keep ruling you out....*
*and*
*you have to keep proving them wrong....*

□

# Recreating Beginner's Luck

## It all Begins with Beginner's Luck

It is a small easy victory that starts it all. I tend to meet a lot of many people who keep grumbling that it was so easy the first time around. It is just like gambling, where sometimes because of beginner's stroke of luck you win a small sum in the starting and that seduced you to lose more money.

Yes, it tends to get more difficult and testing as we go forward. More realistic. Some people learn, some people remain in the beautiful illusion of that first win and fail to understand why the magic is not recurring.

One of the reasons for this phenomenon is that when you play for the first time there is nothing to lose and you have little pressure. Also you are more experimental as compared to an expert who is more likely to play in a restricted pattern.

## How to Recreate the Beginner Luck?

Play as if there is nothing to lose.

Try new and unconventional strategies.

Remember, success has two phases: initial may be a

result of beginner's luck but latter phase needs diligence, grit and strategy.

But then, if we hadn't been lucky the first time around who knows we may not have dared to have go down this road at all.

□

## Bird of Success

**This picture has been the answer to most of the questions in life for me. I hope this answers your questions as well.**

In this picture, you will see a beautiful bird. The bird symbolizes desire. Beautiful but difficult to achieve. It can be your next degree, your exam, relationship, next promotion, new car whatever. Hand symbolizes the path to achieve it.

Some people take it easy; they hold the bird too lightly. They are the easy going type. They want to win but they don't want to work hard over it. Their bird falls.

Some people take it too hard; they make it a matter of life and death. They try so hard that they end up squeezing the bird. Their bird is crushed under the weight of their expectation.

***Art of success is holding the bird firmly, not so lightly that it falls and not so hard that it crushes.***

□

## Drive

Do you feel the need to go forward or are you satisfied with status quo? Interestingly, there are people who exist and there are people who have the drive. Drive needs fuel. It is fuelled by passion, ardent desire to win, feeling the moment of glory with the adrenaline surge. Drive needs the will to work for passion, need to be in "no regrets" phase. Find what drives you to push your own boundaries. Beyond talent, beyond intelligence, beyond smartness, success is linked to your drive. Drive is not for money, or for avoiding failure. It is an intrinsic need to achieve something worthwhile which pushes you to stretch your limits.

*Do you have the 'drive'?*

□

## Don't Ask Me to Dream Logically

To reach somewhere its imperative to know about the place first. When you get to know about a place, you find it appealing then you find a way to reach there. Same goes for success, find what you want, learn more about it or read about it. Chase your interest and you will find a way to reach there. Being realistic or conformist will not lead to new ideas. Sometimes your success is limited by your capacity to think rather than talent.

*Think big, dream unreal, try to go beyond horizon beyond limits.*

□

## Smell of Victory

*Strange are the ways of the world.*

People who lose don't know how to win. Losing hope instead of stimulus work harder, acts as a vicious circle and they get more and more negative and they end up with a serial repetition of loses.

On the other hand, what is the secret of winners, they work when they smell victory. A tiny sentinel win, which otherwise would seem nothing extraordinary, stimulates them to do extraordinary effort. They can subconsciously perceive the faint idea of winning.

You don't put extraordinary effort when you lose, although stories make you think that is the case. In real life, you need to get the sense of impending win.

*That's the smell of victory. That's the most potent and best stimulus.*

□

# Fake Contentment

Some people stick to fake contentment to hide their inability to go forward. They use their apparently satisfactory contentment statements to hide their inherent laziness, their resistance to change. Desire for change to adapt better with the nature is inbuilt in our evolution system. Nature desires change. Contentment cannot be used as a defence mechanism against failure. True contentment comes with desire to evolve, to do more with life and lead a fuller life. You can always ask why should I fight more, why should I do more with life? Why is maintaining the status quo not enough?

*Answer lies is in this famous quote, "A ship is safe in harbor, but that's not what ships are for."*

*Fight stagnation, live your life, surviving is just not enough.*

□

## No Regrets

What do you think affects us more, failure or regret? Regret is more painful, I believe. Tiny little regret that you feel when you don't do what you should have done just because you were afraid of losing, afraid of failures and risks pains you all the more.

Initially, I used to be afraid of failure and often didn't do things I believed in and instead of chasing things by heart's after, I would always try to be rational and appear logical. Then, when you see someone doing what you wanted to do, you regret. That is more painful than losing. Idea of life, exams, business and relationships is simple, you need to gather enough nerve to follow your dream and do things that you really want to do with all passion and energy you can put in. Results won't matter in the end, but if you have done all you could you will have no regrets and be at peace with yourself. You will be wiser with experience and more doors will open up. Probably, that is the sportsman spirit as well, you want to win every game, when you play, you play to win, you play as if life depends on the game but if you lose, there are no regrets as you played with all you had. If regrets are allowed to accumulate, you become someone you promised yourself you would never be, someone who lived his life being safe and full of self-pity.

I do ask myself this question over all decisions, will I regret not doing this, if yes then let's take a chance. I may still lose but at least I will have no regrets. Trust me these are most relevant two words you would want to write on the last page of your autobiography....

**As rightly said by J.K. Rowling, "It is impossible to live without failing at something, unless you live so cautiously that you might as well not have lived at all-in which case, you fail by default."**

□

# Cut the Ropes

What is holding you back?

- your fear of failure
- your insecurities
- your prejudices and vanity
- expectations
- others' opinions
- self-doubts

You want to fly but you are tied down by self-made ropes.

These ropes will open the day you realise that your time is limited and you decide that you would rather fail trying than regretting not trying at all.

That's freedom. To chase your dreams and do things which others think improbable.

*Introspect, find your ropes, cut them and liberate yourself.*

*Strange are the ways of the ropes more you think about them, tighter they get, ignore them and you go free.... Detachment...it is.*

□

## Retirement at 40: Myth or Reality

Retirement at 40 myth:

This is something I have heard a lot of people say, "we will work till 40 and then enjoy the remainder."

Sounds interesting, but is it really true? Do you think life comes with guaranteed years? We sacrifice our "present" for uncertain, yet to reveal the future. Moreover, what if we retire at 40 years of age, it would be so boring. Life is neither about overworking nor about retiring. Life is about enjoying what you do and balancing the "life-work-family balance". Life is about evolving your roles with time and enjoying your role each phase of life.

Years back I used to believe that a perfect job would be no work and good money and when I finally found a job like this, I resigned within two months. Management asked me why do you want to leave, we will increase your salary and incentives, still I couldn't get myself challenged enough to continue. Gradually, I realized that it was not work that was pulling me down, rather I needed to work for myself, my ideas, and I needed creative freedom and finally left my job, not to be free from work, but to work even harder with a new found passion and energy.

***It is not about retiring one day, it is not about finally living some day and more so it is about living each day.***

□

## Fears and Dreams

We are so used to the status quo. Change scares us. Even if the present is not what we want from life, we cling onto it. We are afraid what if we lose this as well.

We tremble because "fear of the unknown. We have this tremendous desire of giving up. Let's not go ahead. Let's not risk the present.

### What if We Lose?

*Dreams require faith, faith to overcome fear. Faith to let it go. Faith to fall freely.*

Do something today that you always wanted to but was not sure of its worth it.

It may be a small desire or life time dream. You may win, you may lose.

*But the process of going for it sets you free and that is all that matters.*

□

## Was this it?

There is always something to aim for. Better house, better lifestyle, better car, in short, we are always striving for a better quality of life.

He worked towards the next target, with all his ability and would often achieve things much before his peers could. All his life he kept looking at the mountain and was always preoccupied by the thought of conquering the peak. He wanted to be on the top of the world.

His only trouble was, whenever he reached a so-called milestone, people around him would be amazed and his feeling always would be:

*Was this it?*

*We all sometimes give it all to reach somewhere, in pursuit of achieving something and surprising thing is often when we reach there, we feel confused as we are not feeling as exhilarated as expected.*

*Haven't we all at times on reaching the peak of proverbial mountain felt, "was this it?"*

□

## Madness

*There is no fun in life until and unless someone calls you mad.*

When you love madly, you love unconditionally and irrevocably.

When normal gets boring and you take pride in being the "abnormal" one.

As rightly said by Dr. House: "Normal is often overrated."

You love the moon, you like looking up the sky and firmly believe that's the place for you up there.

When world is racing past, and calls you insane for standing still and you wonder who is the mad one... for it is **"better to have a sore neck for aiming too high than to have a moustache for aiming too low."**

Yes, they will call you mad, but isn't the touch of madness being part of being alive.

*Madness is being able to see the world as it is while the sane ones see it as they want to see....*

□

## Consistency is the Key

It is ok to take risk taker and take it in a gambler's way. It is ok to be bit defensive and have a risk averse approach to life.

You will meet successful ones of either type and it does not matter if you are risk taker or risk averse type as long as you are consistent in your efforts towards goal.

Because if you keep with your approach, life will throw at you some jackpot and some wrong cards and if you are consistent, eventually odds of winning will average out.

*Only important thing is to be consistent.*

*Don't become a risk taker all of a sudden. Occasional gamblers loose more.*

*And if risk taking is your forte and you are at the verge of victory, become risk averse you will miss the fortune.*

**"The only time success comes before work is in dictionary," as said by Harvey Specter (suits CBS TV show).**

□

# LEADERSHIP

## Sculpturing and Leadership

Things don't reach their final stage in one step. And I may say there is nothing like a final, perfect stage. You cannot hope for things to be perfect in one go.

Leadership or success in life is a constant endeavour of sculpturing. You have to keep shaping and carving it. You feel you have reached the final stage then just like the artist, you notice yet another small imperfection and you've to chisel it to perfection.

Look at your role as a sculptor who with his soft hands shapes and carves constantly. Sometimes you need to use a bit more pressure, and sometimes even a soft nudge does.

Nature also does the same with natural selection.

One who claims that he has reached the best, he could has already begun his downfall. Nature favours the constant sculptors.

□

## Nitpicking Kills the Team

*Nitpicking is defined as a concern with insignificant details, especially with the intention of finding fault.*

We all have met 'nitpickers' before. You tell them the entire story and you feel you have explained the crux of the message and they will point out a grammatical mistake. You finish a big project and they will point out the lack of cleanliness of the office. Tiny and insignificant.

As long as nitpicker is in a junior position, it hardly matters. Problem arises when nitpickers acquire leading positions in organizations and teams. They have this habit of diverting from the bigger picture and focus on puny irrelevant details. They will find fault with people and many of those would be actually doing a good job if you consider the bigger picture.

*Good leaders have this ability of deviating from it and focusing on more significant details and becoming the eagle when required and soar high in the sky to look at the bigger picture.*

□

# Google's New CEO: One More for the 'Argumentative' Ones

*Sundar Pichai has been named CEO of Google by the company's founders Larry Page and Sergey Brin. And the debate ensues on why talented people from India go abroad. Same question, I have heard many times as a doctor, why young doctors go abroad? Why don't they work in their own nation?*

However, I would beg to differ.

We need to think of the world today as a hyperlinked flat world, and it is governed by a fiercely competitive "demand and supply" chain. National boundaries are now more of geopolitical interest, while, world of trade and information technology is single hyper-connected unit, where resources, both material and human, are sourced from places of abundance to places of need.

To retain talent, as a society in general, we have to look towards building a structure of meritocracy in the organizations, give the creative people the freedom to create their ideas and create a culture of intra-organizational entrepreneurship.

If, as a nation, we take care of the talented and

creative people, give them the environment they strive for, the battle is half won.

*Let's stop debating.*

*If we don't give respect and place to people who deserve, someone else will.*

□

## Role You Play

As you progress in life, you evolve at work too and so does your role. People and circumstances expect you to enact that role. Often, I see people stuck in their previous roles while the situation demands something else and becomes the limiting factor for their and their teams' success.

We have all heard about people who fail to grow up and team leaders who fail to evolve from earlier positions.

Good people may make not so good leaders if they don't identify what is expected from them now and enact accordingly. Remember even in cricket great players don't make a good captain.

*You cannot afford to be a "soldier" when the war needs you to be the 'general'.*

□

# Friction

When we plan our work or life, our plans are based on a perfect world. A perfect world has no friction. Just like in science, they made laws of science ignoring friction, they sounded perfect, but could not explain reality.

Similarly, when we start implementing our ideas, things which we never anticipated begin to happen. They slow you down. They appear trivial but they hold you back. Perfect plans seemingly become imperfect when you start implementing. You begin to see flaws in your plans. They are not completely compatible with reality as you would've initially thought.

This is real life. It is not perfect. It has friction.

Art of winning is knowing by experience that friction exists and make room for it your plans.

□

# Seeing from Others' Side Their Perspective

Same questions seem to have different answers when they apply to us or to others. When it comes to others' lives, everyone seems to know what is to be done. But when it comes to our own lives same questions appear unanswerable and the fine line between right and wrong appears blurred. We all tend to go into a judgmental phase when the situation is about others. But, when you are supposed to take a call on your own self, it is a different ball game altogether.

We all have a perception about ourselves, which in part is 'factual' and in part 'made belief' by which we round off rough edges of our own self-image to create a perfect self-image and we judge others with respect to this 'perfect' image of ours.

There is no such thing as a perfect 'human'. We all judge people and their circumstances based on our own self-image and experiences in life.

*There is no such thing as absolute 'right' or 'wrong', there are just people, perspectives and circumstances.*

□

# The Perfect Team with Perfect People: Myth or Reality

Loads of time is spent or I would say rather wasted by people and organizations to recruit the best people and hire the 'perfect' people for the job. Many people believe if you get the right people suited for job and get the best in each department, you become inconvincible. Does it really work that way? My own belief and experience is to the contrary. You cannot hire 11 Sachin Tendulkars and master the IPL.

**Valid reasons for this theory are:**

(1) Sachin (× 11) would be too expensive a proposition and likelihood of viability and profitability are much lesser. Especially for a start up.

(2) There is always a risk involved that so many perfect people will have ego problems and fixity of ideas which may not allow them to act together like a team. They are less likely to follow the captain's (CEO) vision with young contagious enthusiasm.

(3) The competition too knows the weaknesses of each other and entire team collapses, because

they all are predictable all being similar in numerous aspects.

(4) Most important reason that such scenarios don't work is the "mismatch". When you are just starting your system or your organization is young; you are bound to be less than perfect and if you employ all "perfect" people, the relationship will not last long as perfect people would seek more perfect employment opportunities.

So, my radical thought of the day is, when hiring somebody, just look at the broad possibility of an overall "fit" in your system. Start up systems evolve with time and role of people working with you will evolve and gradually they will fit into their rightful niches. It is the role of the captain or the CEO to keep the people in their suited dynamic niche which has to be changed from time to time. As their job evolves, their roles should also evolve, and usually the best "fit" in the organization are the ones who grow with the company.

*Perfect team is not made of perfect people, rather it is bunch of imperfect people (including CEO) who synchronize together to build a perfect team.*

☐

## Secret to Success: Put Others First

Do you really want to be successful?

Then actually stop thinking about success and make decisions from others' perspectives in mind. That's the secret of life, people want to win and keep thinking of themselves, while success lies in being able to keep other person's interest in mind. Associate people with you and those who come in contact with you and those who win without selfish interests and you will emerge even more successful. Try being self-centred and you will end being overrated average manager. That's the difference between managers and leaders. Leaders keep everyone's interest in mind and they are sought after as CEO(s) of top firms. Organizations get stuck with self-centred managers while leaders help their firms become better and make a proper team working with everyone together for each other.

*If you strive to become a leader then strive to make everyone a winner, keep other person's interest at priority and you will become their priority. That's the secret....*

□

## Different 'Worlds'

'World' has a different meaning for each one of us. We all live in our own worlds, with us in the centre and a circumference of people and 'world' which matters to us. There are 'other worlds' coexisting with our worlds and we fail to acknowledge them until they overlap with ours. You progress when you are able to understand what it feels to be in 'other worlds'. The best leaders are those who have risen to high ranks from the bottom and their life has seen multiple worlds on the way.

*Just for instance, we as doctors see hospital from an entirely different perspective and if we ever go to the same hospital as a patient, it is a different world altogether. You see places in the hospital which you never noticed earlier and learn things that you never would have. That is when you evolve into physician as a human being.*

□

## People Change

All this while we all kept talking about adapting to the changing environment, changing climate or changing economy, while we forgot the most important change that is constant happening to us and around us. "We Change, People Change". We are not the same person that we were 10 years back and changes to our self have been a result of numerous small and large experiences and events during this time frame. Why is this important to realize?

Because sometimes you may know a person at one stage of his/her life and then you keep correlating that person's self with that initial image. Consequently, failing to understand them in their present self. This happens because you are trying to understand and perhaps judge a changed person, by your impression of them which is no more true. That is the essence of relationship building, personal and professional both, adaption to present self of the other people. Big organizations are created by people who keep adapting to new 'self' of the employees and clients, who are bound to change. Innumerable times does one hear employees complaining that their boss still treats them like a newcomer. Numerous times one can see young adults complaining that their parents still treat them like kids. Yes, people change, they acquire skills, confidence, experience of loss/win and they gradually change into a new self, adaption to which is an important life skill. Let's not always become biased by the past image that you had formed initially and learn to see people as they are in their present.

You may choose to see them through your 'green' glasses.

But people change and so do the circumstances.

□

## Team Building and 'Temple Run'

You work hard to reach the next level but when you get there, you get trapped in zone full of preconceived notions about workflow and petty issues which appear to be insurmountable. If you don't rise to the occasion, you get tied down to that level for ages. People who do really well are people who keep moving to the next level by clearing the dogmas and breaking free of preconceived notions, and work by delegating and team building.

Most people do well to certain level then they get anchored down and overcrowded. They become prisoners of the house they had created. Their insecurity doesn't allow them to trust people and they get stuck. Way to rise higher is paradoxical and most important factor that defines superlative success is team building. Business is like the game 'temple run' – you have to keep running forward or you are captured.

□

# HANDLING FAILURE

## Take Help,
## Seek Other's Perspective

Sometimes we all hit a block, we all hit the 'bottom' and anybody can go wrong at times. Many of us are afraid to allow others to give us an insight into our problems because it makes us feel vulnerable. Insecurity and ego are other issues holding us back. However, sometimes what is obvious to everyone else is invisible to the sufferer. Because, the other person might be able to give an unbiased comment and a clearer view of things.

*Let me quote Gibran here, "Is not the mountain far more awe-inspiring and more clearly visible to one passing through the valley than to those who inhabit who inhabit the mountains?"*

□

## Hanging On

Have you ever felt that life is unfair? Have you ever done all you could do and still you've lost. Contrary to your thoughts when you deserved to win still you lost. Yes, it is true that sometimes you lose despite playing well, despite all the hard work you've put because this is part and parcel of life. This wasn't told at school. They said if you work hard you will win, but success is never so mathematical. Never so rational.

*Question is "Then what do you do when you lose despite giving in all that you had?"*

You feel lost and dejected. I will give you the answer; which probably is the secret of winners, it is as simple as this "**they hang on**". Yes, even if they are unable to go "full throttle" immediately, they hold on. That is what you need to do, life may seem unfair at the moment but remember to hang on and the path will show up again. Every game has equal probability of winning or losing, and you may still lose despite putting in the best, but the way forward is to hang on and get back to track.

*It may take a while, it may look uphill, life may appear unfair but the winners hang on.*

***"Life is fair in being unfair."***

□

# The Moment When You Almost Gave it Up

There are times when things seem to go wrong, there are times when we feel we are not able to force things to happen. That's when we give up and change the course. Then at times you question yourself "what would have happened if you had stayed held back?" and regret follows. Some people win, some people lose, they both at one point of time felt the same urge to give it up at 'that moment' but winners continue to endure the pain of uncertainty and overcome the fear of failure, and stay put. That's what is courage and that is what separates winners from losers. Yes, need of the moment was to stay put, not trying to move forward. Courage is not always forcing forward, sometimes it means staying put despite odds and the moment you give up, you lose the battle. It was actually a test to scare the weak away and you got scared.

*As Edison said: "The most certain way to succeed is always to try just one more time."*

□

## Invisible Walls

This is something that I often feel, we all are surrounded by transparent invisible walls, which are usually transparent to us and we surpass them even without noticing them. But to some people these walls are opaque and they get stuck. Take for example: exams. Most people pass them for walls to them are transparent, but every year you see some people getting stuck up. Same analogy goes for most of the things in life, I have met people who had it easy all the way along be it getting into medical school, a job or into a relationship – **'transparent walls'** as I say, actually didn't exist for them. They didn't even feel any obstacle at all, yet somehow some people get stuck and for them walls become opaque. Paradoxically, more intensely and obsessively the person hits at the **'now opaque'** wall, more he gets bounced back. Art of crossing **'THE WALL'** is to be sure enough, be prepared enough and still not making it a matter big enough when it comes to life and death. "Walls remain opaque if you take them too easy or you make them an obsession". When you want something and you are detached from the end consequence, that 'opaque' wall again becomes transparent. Another thing to learn from it is 'humility' and understanding others. What you think as easy, may not be so for someone else.

Respect the wall, respect diversity and you will learn the art to cross the 'invisible'.

Did you ever encounter any wall which others thought was non-existent and how did you deal with it?

□

## Courage

Although we all have been taught about courage in school, yet what exactly does courage mean in our day-to-day life or is it just limited to the soldiers in the war or warriors who exhibit such feeling. To me courage is about the choice to move forward even when odds are against you and you always can give up. We all get the option to be courageous with our choices or to give up. Trust me, everybody experiences the fear of failure, everyone feels like giving up at sometime, but the winners chose to go forward.

*Sometimes even staying put needs courage and moving forward needs conviction in your dreams. That's the secret of winners, they chose to face the consequences of their actions.*

□

## Quitters

There are always people who give up too soon. They join a new job and next day, they say, they have not been given due opportunities and they quit again. They are impatient. Then there are people who give up on challenges, relationships too soon. There are students who start studying and give up. I don't mean to say that you hold on to impossible situations, but at least give yourself some time and think it over again before you decide to quit.

Most important factor that determines success is persistence and constant desire to succeed. Successful people take time to commit to a cause, but then they are stubborn. They hold on. Initial phase is always testing, but their persistence takes them it to the next level. It is not about talent, not about luck, but it is about grit and determination.

*Remember: Winners never quit, and those who quit never win.*

□

## The Other Side of the Story

**Winner's perspective:** All his life he kept looking at the world with his own perspective. To him that was the only view possible. World was a sphere for him with no walls. This sphere was his perception of the world and he actually never thought that world could exist outside his sphere of perception. He was winning and there was no reason for him to suspect that anything else could be true.

**The other side:** Then one day he lost. Yes, he lost significantly. He was no longer a successful man any longer. He started seeing things from a loser's perspective. He could see the other side of the coin. Same situations, same people around but with changed perspectives. May be he needed a jolt to see the other side of the story. May be we all need one defeat to open up our sphere of life.

***Opening the doors:*** *Losing the battle opens new perspectives which we never even noticed while we were on a winning spree.*

*As it is popularly said: There are always three sides to a story; yours, theirs, and the truth.*

□

## Winners Tell a 'Modified' Story

*Who knows if they are just fitting the pieces to make a story once the end is known.*

After the battle is won, the General describes the war with story of the bravery of his soldiers. Story would never include their weak moments, moments of cowardice, moments of questions, moments of uncertainty and moments when they almost gave up.

*Yes, winners though unintentionally change the story to make it all sound like a well-planned mission.*

□

## What not to Do When You are Feeling Low

We all have tendency to crib and cry when we are down. When things are not going our way, we tend to crib. We look for people who would listen to us. Say nice things to us. They may not always be our well-wishers. Not everyone who listens to you when you are feeling low is your well-wisher.

This is where sometimes we open gates to outsiders to our internal affairs. More negative we say, more negativity we attract.

Not only that we end up ignoring our well-wishers who may be more straightforward in putting facts to us.

We start to seek sympathy, we look to people who will listen to our story.

And things start to go the spiral way.

**Always remember:**

*Things may not be right at the moment, but stay positive. More you radiate optimism, more you attract success back to you.*

*People who listen to you and say "sugar coated" words are not always the well-wishers and well-wishers aren't always nice. It is necessary to take feedback from people who matter, trust them and look up to it to bring a positive change.*

Category: Handling Failure

Three most powerful words: "It is possible" remember even impossible expands into "I (a)m possible."

"It is possible". You never know the value and power of these words till that moment of despair and defeat arrives and someone looks into your eyes and says "it is possible" and ignites the fire again. Sometimes all you need is an assurance and when you get it you are in the right direction to set the ball rolling. It has capacity to turn the air of negativity into optimism.

Often

*It all starts with the phrase; "**it is possible.**"*

□

## One Day a Miracle will Occur

I have a firm belief that we all usually know what is wrong in our lives, works and relationships. But somehow we don't try to look for an answer and rather wait for a miracle to happen. Somehow, we know what is to be done yet we keep ignoring the 'inner voice' and the 'bitter truth' and try escaping from it.

We just want someone from "above to come" and solve our problems. That is our expectation from leader as well. We all know what is wrong, but we want someone to rub the magic lamp and solve it in a jiffy. Interesting thing.

We always know, it is just that we chose to ignore.

We all wish "one day a miracle would occur" and we keep postponing the obvious for the miracle.

Unfortunately, there are no miracles till the time you get up and take control of the situation. There is a price to be paid for everything.

*Sometimes hope and despair blinds you from the obvious, but deep down.... You always know....*

□

## Best Teacher in Life – Failure

People often underestimate the value of occasional failure in life. I think it is often the turning point for many. Imagine, if you were just winning, winning and winning all the time, you will never ever know the value of victory, you will never be able to put the same intense effort every time for you don't have the dejection of losing. You just cannot have it easy all the time and yet have the hunger, the desire and the fire to win. I sincerely believe you should win some, you lose some. You get charged by winning but you get to know the true value only when you lose. That is the life's way of teaching you, you get to know where you went wrong and more than that you get to explore a new path altogether. It makes you humble, and enables you to value sweet taste of victory when it comes. It is all about taking failure positively, and learning from it, and realizing that even best people lose at times and make mistakes. It is not winning that makes someone great. It is learning from mistakes which creates the 'magic'. Sometimes you just have to fail to succeed... fall to spring back.

□

## Experience

When he lost the game for the first time, he felt it was all over. He thought he was not worth it.

He asked his coach, coach asked him to hold on, he said it will pass.

He did not understand. But repeated the words like a mantra. It will pass. And yes, bad times did pass.

He played for years together and many times a situation came when he thought it was all over. He was blank. But just kept repeating "it will pass."

He never understood the phrase but somehow it seemed to work for him and bad times passed.

Years later, he left active sport and worked as a coach for young players, one promising youngster walked up to him and said he could not take it any longer and felt like quitting. He reverted back to him and said "it will pass."

And that was moment of truth for the coach.

That is all he had learnt from experience.

*Things pass.*

□

# The Ones Who Lag Behind

## School

*She always thought she was superior to her batch mates. She was decent looking and till now had been doing quite well in her class. She was second to none in her eyes and she had no reason to believe it elsewise. It was her dream to get into the best college of the city and no one else other than her deserved to be in that dream college.*

## College

Based on her merit she got admission in to the top most college of city.

At first, it looked like school.

But with every passing day, she started feeling as if she was lagging behind the rest.

Her colleagues were apparently more intelligent than hers, they seem to answer the teacher's questions with ease. She tried harder, and more she tried, less she remembered.

Then, there were the flashy ones in the class. She started to fall behind in grades, she lagged behind all the more it started a vicious cycle for her.

She tried to look different. More she tried, worse the results got. She lost confidence to make friends and was often with her own self. She began talking to herself.

Parents could not understand her downfall. No one noticed her despair.

She wanted to conform. Yet, she was not meant to be one. Finally, had to drop out of the college and no one heard of her after that. Actually, no one even bothered. They did not even notice her absence.

*Schools and colleges represent dreams of many. But the pursuit of dreams very quickly turns competitive. You have to run to keep pace or risk being left behind. Some manage to conform and be a part of tribe. Some manage to carry their originality.*

*But yes some are left behind.*

*Do we ever bother?*

□

# WINNER'S SECRET

## Success has a Price to be Paid

Many people want to be successful or want to win in their pursuits, be it exams, business or life, but only a handful of them are successful. Simple reason is the fact that there is a price to be paid in terms of sacrificing leisure, sleep or sometimes even sacrificing your entire comfort zone. Many are success hungry but too lazy, too reluctant to pay the price and blame their bad luck which is the easiest scapegoat. You lose because you simply are too lazy to follow your dream and you don't want to take risk or put the bet on yourself. You look for safe options and blame luck in the end. If you are looking for a magic formula and hoping it to work, trust me, odds are against you. Think of athletes, sportsmen they sacrifice most of their childhood practicing which you spend watching TV. I have heard many people complain that cricketers get it easy, is it so? I meet so many people every day and many are curious, many have ideas but only a few with intent and drive to convert thoughts to action. Simply put "to win there are prices to be paid". I will quote "THE MOST QUOTED", "there is nothing like a free lunch."

□

## When You Doubt Your Power, You Give Power to Your Doubt

There is one major difference between people who win and people who don't. People who do well generally don't doubt their abilities. While people who lose, are often plagued by self-doubts. These self-doubts can be multi-factorial and usually are as a result of previous failures. Problem with self-doubt is that it creates a sense of negativity in our approach and you begin to question your own abilities. When confronted with this parasite of self-doubt from within, your resolve to succeed weakens and downfall begins.

*As the famous quote by Honore de Balzac goes, "When you doubt your power, you give power to your doubt."*

Everyone in some stage of their life doubts, and when I face self-doubt, I try to bring back positivity into my work by few simple techniques which I feel will help others as well. Simplest way is to take a break from routine and do something creative. For me it is writing my heart out. Another approach is I try to avoid negative people and I surround myself with positive people, positive literature and yes, I do something which gets me appreciated. Nothing works more than appreciation to boost the morale.

*Battles are often lost not by strength of the enemy, but often because of their own self-doubts. Often, it is not just your ability but your attitude that matters on the "**D**" day of your life.*

□

## Rhythm and Momentum: Winner's Secret Tools

***Analogy to football Match**: He could hear his own heartbeat. He knew this was his chance. Momentum was in his favour. He had to strike hard and strike fast. Crowd was cheering. Cheering was giving him the rhythm and it all seemed to be happening in a flash. That was the big moment.*

Competition is always tough. You can never be sure of winning as you can only plan for it to happen, other side is always unpredictable and a variable beyond your control. All work hard but forget the power of rhythm, and momentum in competitive sports and exams there by underestimating it.

**Rhythm:** Venus Williams once said, "The thing about tennis is if you stay off for two weeks, or just for three days, you can lose your rhythm quickly. So it's just a question of constant diligence and vigilance."

This is exactly what happens to students who take a gap in studies and then lose the entire rhythm and their performance falls by a great margin.

**Momentum:** Success comes from taking the initiative and holding onto it. Work hard, work with full energy and intensity and just be passionate about it. Let the momentum build, it creates the force that helps to beat any threshold and achieve what you have dreamt of.

***The Secret:*** *Start with small actions, gain rhythm, repeat, gain momentum and it will carry you. When you feel the rhythm in your work and you feel the momentum building, you know you are almost there.*

□

## Power of 'The Moment'

Radical thought yet again. I have always felt that more I think about something; more complex it becomes. And usually I end up doing what I always knew I would. Do we actually overrate thinking? I have a firm belief that every time we face a confusing situation, for a fraction of a second we are lost we know what we really want but then it gets clouded by reality and thinking. It happens in competitive exams as well. I have had the good fortune for getting a single digit rank in many exams. And had the chance of interacting with many top rankers because of DAMS. Most of the top rankers knew the answers all of them yes all of them. Similarly, many business leaders when questioned why were they into this domain, they just knew it. They knew why they were there. This happens many times in personal life as well, you know what you really want but you keep clouding your thinking. Even in business while making decisions I have learnt, many people think too much and end up doing nothing and many of those are a result of gut feeling.

For a brief moment, you always know what you want; all you need is the ability to tap into that hidden wisdom, that divine signal, to know what is to be done. Learn to hear your own voice and God willing, you will get to hear the best advice you have ever heard.

Amen!

□

## Passionate Yet Detached

This is my mantra to success and will sound paradoxical to most of you.

Most entrepreneurs are definitely passionate about their work for sure but very few are able to detach themselves from it. I always wondered why top business leaders like Steve Jobs also developed their spiritual side and I am sure many of you won't understand this. Now with years of being engrossed in my work, my passion with medical education and technology, I have gradually understood the art of **'detached passion'**. Sometimes overtly passionate leaders get involved in tiny things which actually don't deserve their valuable time and attention and get involved into everything along the way, missing the bigger picture. Secondly, people are quiet preoccupied with concern about the returns and rewards all the time, they are important no doubt, but until and unless you detach yourself from the returns and results, and focus on getting yourself on **'your'** road, the road that you want to travel in life, you will not evolve into true leader. Organizations need leaders who are passionate to the core sticking to values and mission of the company, yet detached enough to see what is happening from the correct perspective. Detached still passionate leaders are able to take tough calls and then business goes beyond winning and losing, beyond profits and losses; where eventually entrepreneurship and spirituality merge.

□

## Meaning of Success

There are many people who define success in terms of money, power or fame but the question remains the same. It's a question to self, "have I made it big enough to stop":

For me success is as follows:

**Work:** You may call yourself successful, when while you are working you feel the joy and are practically detached from everything and just lost in it. I have seen great doctors, surgeons, teachers, artists at work. Children think "isn't it too boring to do the same work over and again. But that is what successful people do, they attain so much perfection in their work that when they are working they feel the divine joy of working towards perfection. Their each performance is a step towards improvement over the last but the audience doesn't see minute adjustments that have been made. While working if you have your moments of divinity and you feel good after each day YOU are successful. Your legs will hurt and your body will be tired but heart will know the joy of work and that will be ultimate success.

**Love:** If you experience moments in love where nothing else matters and is unconditional, you are successful. Trust me you are.

If you have both these components in "life" and "work" which feels like meditation and "love" which is unconditional, you can call yourself successful, it is not about money not about power not about fame, it's about how you live your life.

Amen!!

□

## Insecurity, Expectations and Freedom

Modern life can be defined as sum total of the relationships we cultivate. Family, work and leisure are nothing but a sum total of the web of relationships we create. There are components to relationships which are often not talked about.

***Insecurity:*** *Every moment we have to confront our fears and concerns about inferiority. About our looks, our dressing, being poor or being rich. We all are insecure in some ways, but denying it is the root of most problems. Accept it and life becomes better for you and others around you. Everyone has insecurities just little different from others.*

***Expectations:*** *You have expectations from people and people have expectations from you. Mismatch between expectations and "what you give" (reality) brings dissatisfaction. My two cents are that I keep my expectations low and I always try to deliver more than I promise.*

***Freedom:*** *Every relationship needs space as much as it asks for commitment. Be it your office, home anywhere for that matter, we need to understand just like you need freedom to be yourself, other people also need "IT" to be themselves; besides the fact that they are with you at that time they just need that "little" space. Mind it.*

□

## 'Mediocrity' is Easy

Some people want to stay in the 'zone of mediocrity'; they want to have an easy mediocre life. Mediocrity is easy there is nothing great about it. Lot of talented men who lack enthusiastic approach for future prefer being 'average' just because of ease of being so.

It is the desire for excellence which brings the out that 'extraordinary' of ordinary people, which helps them to "rise to the occasion", play more than their abilities and talent. When you do things that you want to do, be what you want to be, when you are being yourself without pretensions and that is where the journey for excellence begins.

While 'mediocrity' is a sin. It lures you to itself and kills your dreams and passion. You end up being a safe, a riskless mediocre like others lost among many.

*It is just too easy to be a mediocre. It is '**contagious**'. It spreads, spreads and spreads people feel security in mediocrity.*

Safe in '**their comfort**' zones.

*Safe, secure yet mediocre....*

Is that all you want to be known for? For being a mere mediocre.

□

## Despite All the 'Odds'

*Successful people had it easy. They were lucky. Its only me who has got all the problems. If I had no problems, I would have made it big.*

If you think like I have just said, I think you need to re-evaluate your stance towards life. Everyone has their own share of odds. Yes, no one gets it easy, everyone has to pay the price. Some people want success but are unwilling to pay the price. Winners kind of blind out the odds and fear of failure, and create the so-called 'luck' by standing against all the odds tossing everything that comes along.

*Beauty of life and the passion of the warriors is revealed in our day-to-day life when we see ordinary people confronting extraordinary odds with grace and courage.*

□

## Road Less Travelled

At times my students would ask me (in a not so confident tone) I want to do this (book or course), but no one else I know is doing this, should I still pursue the same? My answer to them is: if you want something that most people don't get to have, you have to do something which you feel strongly is made for you and you don't need to wait for their approval. If you keep conforming to the majority, you remain a part of the majority and majority do not reach to top (any exam). This holds true for almost everything else in life as well. To win big, you have to take risk by taking "the road less travelled". There are **'unknown unforeseen'** risks on such roads and unfortunately there are no past records to guide you, but there you are, on your own, on the path less travelled by. All you have is your gut feeling, your instinct to guide your path. That's the thrill of choosing such a path. Few people have the ability to take risks while many of them are happy in being the sheep and thereby following the herd. Sheep looks for safety not for glory. The same holds true about leadership, leaders cannot be afraid of change, they need to constantly look to reinvent the way things are done and find new roads where people don't see any.

If someone asks me what decision has paid me maximum reward in life, it is going to be "the road less travelled."

*As the famous Robert Frost poem goes:*

Two roads diverged in a wood, and I—
I took the one less travelled by,
And that has made all the difference.

□

## Let's Learn to Play to Win in Three Quick Simple Steps

What is the right path to success? What makes winners different?

Here are "my" simple rules:

**(1) Find your road (discover your inner self):** Life throws a lot of options at you and out of these only few are meant for you, rest of them are **'diversions'** or **'blind alleys'** which would lead to a dead end. I personally feel winners find their road early on and that is what helps them to reach farther than others who are still searching searching and searching....

**(2) Initiative:** Many people even when they identify the "path", still hesitate to **'tie the bell'**; they are suspicious of the road and the destination it will lead to. While winners usually have faith and their "idea" to "action" time is least. Faith reduces the lag time which others have because of self-doubts.

**(3) Persistence:** Finally, this is the most important and often under-rated trait of winners; they continue to "persist" despite all the odds. Longer you stay, more you learn from your mistakes and gain experience. They win simply because others gave up just too early.

*In a nut shell, find your call, take initiative and stay put despite the odds....*

□

# The Question is not 'How' but 'Why'

Many people want to do well in some field or the other. People want to do well in their project and their jobs. Some want to perform better in their next exam. They keep looking for ways to achieve that elusive success. They want to discover ways so as to 'how' to do it. They try to learn from other's experiences. But somehow things don't seem to work the way they should.

Probably, the entire question of **"how to do it?"** wasn't just right at first. First question that needs to be answered is **'why'**. If you know **'why'** you want to do something, you will find the way or even better, success will find you.

*Problem is sometimes people keep thinking about 'how' more than the 'why'.*

*The answer lies in the question and question lies in the answer WHY a simple WHY?*

□

## Gap Between 'Saying' and 'Doing'

There are people who say something and act totally opposite to it. Sometimes, people keep saying just to satisfy their inner self-esteem, while they lack the real initiative to take things to next level. It may be because of reasons such as other's opinions or just wanting to have warrior like a self-image. They cling on to certain ambitions while in their heart of heart (they) already know it is a lost cause.

*This lack of synergy between what "we are saying and what we are actually doing is the major reason of failure".*

For instance, people who want to win, but aren't ready to go an extra-mile for it. They keep talking endlessly for days and years together about their desire to win, but all they end up doing is pointing towards some or the other problems stopping them for going out for the goal. Self-doubt is one of the major factors holding them back. They want to be appreciated for their desire but the severe mismatch between what they "preach" and "act" is so obvious to everyone but to themselves that they end up being misjudged by people.

Like people who appear to be always talking about your welfare, and they seem so concerned in their words, but somehow, that doesn't seem to happen. They are just 'saying' for the sake of saying.

*Sometimes, people tend to fool their own self with glorious thoughts while their actions are far from those thoughts.*

*There is nothing more important than being genuinely true to yourself and your intention.*

*You can fool the world but not the one who matters: YOU.*

## Killer Instinct

Sports and competitive exams have a lot in common. In both sports and exams, it is only winning that matters. There is no place for, 'just lost" by a small margin. Similarities don't end here. There is something, which people sometimes miss on superficial analysis. In both you can lose despite playing your best. You can lose even when you did nothing wrong. Competitions don't just depend on whether you are doing right or wrong, they depend on how others play as well. You cannot control the game with your own variables. That is what attracts mankind to the world of competition. Be it sports, exams or business. That inch of uncertainty is the inherent charm of the competitions. **If someone is good you got to be better if someone is better you got to best. If someone is best you got to be better than best.**

*Lionel Messi once said, "**I never think about the play or visualize anything. I do what comes to me at that moment. Instinct. It has always been that way.**"*

Competitions are about two sides and it becomes impossible to predict and plan everything in advance for one side. That is where we have room for instinctive decision making. That is what Messi meant in his famous quote.

The entire phenomenon is difficult to describe in words, it is all about your desire to win, despite knowing you may lose even while playing at your level best and rising to the occasion by playing out of your skin.

*That is what is popularly called as the* ***"Killer Instinct."***

□

## Secret Behind 'Compromise'

Good 'compromise' – most of our life is governed by relations either professional or personal. And yes, we all compromise to meet each other's demands or to adjust according to others moods. But somehow word 'compromise' does not sound something that one would like to do/make.

But, there is something called as a good compromise, where you may 'fall' to meet the needs of other ones but remember without compromising your self-integrity.

Bad 'compromise' – but problem begins when you keep falling even to the extent of compromising 'self' and that is where the trouble begins. Be it job, business relations or personal, principle remains the same.

*In a way everything we do is a compromise between 'their' wish and 'yours'.*

*And as the famous quote by Janis Joplin goes, "Don't compromise yourself. You are all you've got."*

□

## Ability to 'Shut Off' Stress

Most of us believe that winners have it easy. They don't feel the stress. Trust me; everyone does. They too feel the butterflies, just like the popular advertisement: *Darr sabko lagta hai.*

Then, what do winners do, they learn to shut off everything else on '**THE** day'. That might be your exam or a cricket match. You just cannot afford to have a clouded frame of mind on '**THE** day'. It needs to be cleared up. We all have problems in life. We all have limitations and we all have fear of failure. We all have...fears...failures... sadness and happiness.

*People who win are able to shut themselves off from everything else and 'focus' on the task at hand. While people who lose are somehow paralyzed by the fear of failure.*

My way of shutting myself from everything is to do something new that I have been waiting to do since long, that keeps me occupied as all my energy is focused on the 'new' task and then I find myself recharged again for the original 'task' which actually matters. I feel this is the principle behind vacations, you shut yourself from everything and then things start happening. You are able to break the **'jammed'** lock. Some people keep pushing even when their output is not optimal. Remember it's like reading in the library and staring at a single page for hours. They do it because of fear of failure, not because of love of studies.

*When you learn to shut yourself from stress, and fear of failure, victory is yours.*

*Quoting The Alchemist here, "There is only one thing that makes a dream impossible to achieve: the fear of failure."*

□

## Thought to Action – Lag Time

I overheard someone talking about a very successful man and saying that he also had the same brilliant idea.

I interjected and asked him how much worth the idea had.

Many people get ideas, but only few have the 'drive' to convert thoughts to action. And out of those few, only few actually have all the ingredients like leadership, team building and correct timing.

People tend to overrate ideas. They are not worth that much until and unless you reduce the "thought to action" lag. That is what every winner does....

When I introspect:

*That's my fear, that's my drive when I get an idea I get restless, I get sleepless and I want to put it to action before anyone else does and want it to be better than anyone else. That 'feeling' recharges me and I feel most useful when I am possessed by an idea. I feel there is something about this which underlies all scientists, entrepreneurs and artists alike. They get restless with a thought and they want to convert into action.*

□

# Only Change is Permanent

'Stability' is what our mind wants and 'change' is what our heart desires. Most of us from our childhood have been trained to look for a point of stability. You get a stable position, you become a doctor, be afraid of what you don't know and remain in your safe zone defined by limited vision of your young self and family background. My life has been like this, typical background and friend circle, always questioning the need to change and typical desires of stability and safety associated with medical career. My interest in history always attracts me to monuments and then I always wonder why did the king spend so much time and resources to construct the building, while all that people appreciate now is ruins of a once glorious palace. May be they thought if they construct huge, fantabulous structure it will be stable forever, but nothing survives except the change. Things and people change with time, sometimes you keep associating yourself with image of the person you once knew and ignore the obvious that people change and even you are not the same person anymore. Let's learn from nature and every inhabitant of this planet, nature is not looking for stability, but it is looking for change and adaptability to change is best ability to learn in life.

Let's not teach our children to look for safe zones, let us tell them to explore, not be averse to change and be open to new vistas. Create the new world through 'change'.

□

# DECISION MAKING

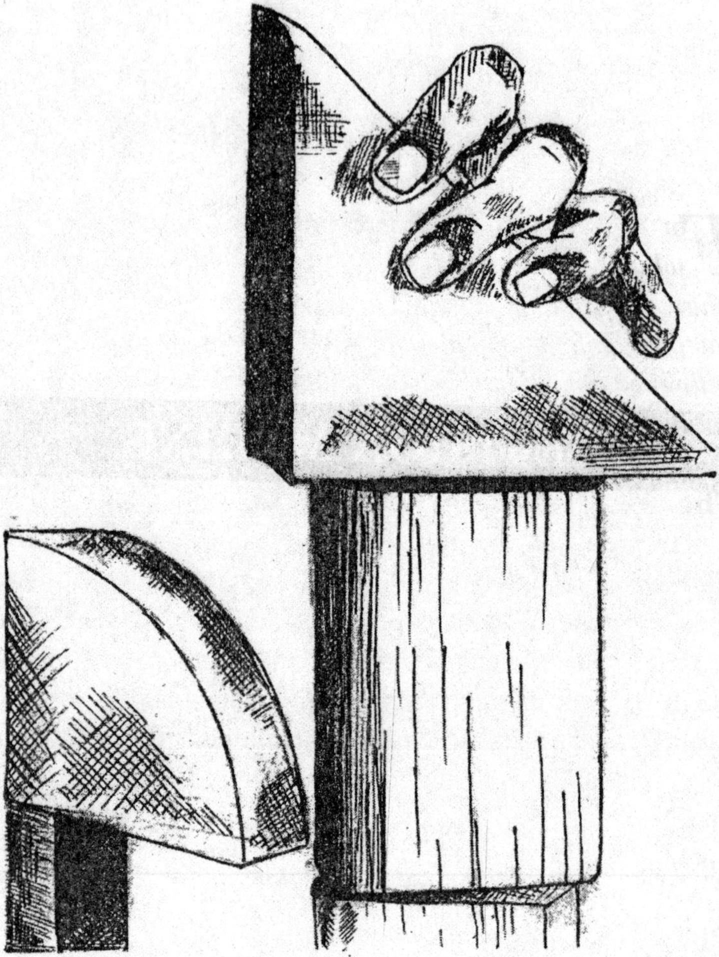

# Choices You Make

*For the sake of clarity let's imagine life as a game in which as you progress you get to face 'decision boxes' where you have to put your hand on 'yes' or 'no' or you can postpone the decision making. Choices you make in life define where you reach in life and what you will end up doing.*

## The Optimist

In this the default setting of player is betting on clicking yes on almost all boxes keeping in mind "faith" that everything that happens is already planned and is happening for good. He does not want to regret not playing. He has the advantage of speed as he doesn't think about pros and cons, and thus gets the lead time over others. He has the disadvantage of being foolhardy at times, and has chances of being betrayed because of his blind faith.

## The Pessimist

He always sees the possibilities of things going wrong and in his default mode chooses not to take the risk. He refuses opportunities because of his inherent scepticism. But he is usually the safe one and often manages to avoid disasters of betrayal which the optimist often faces. His plus point is safety, while his negative would be slow decision making and often losing out the lead time to the optimists.

*Where we find our self in life today is the result of choices we have made in the past. We have to say 'yes' or 'no' to choices available, and these decisions define our path forward.*

*Balancing the two ways of life is the key to happiness in life. The worst thing that you can do in your life is postponing the 'call'. Postponing the 'call' puts us in a vicious loop of regret and failure.*

□

# To Wait for the Dream Bus or Board the One that is Right There in Front of You

Here he was. He was supposed to take the call to join this job as per discussions with people who matter, family and friends. This was not exactly a dream come true but, this was a good compromise. With every passing second his mind came back to the same question, should he take this call or not should he or not. It has been always like this for him. You cannot call him a loser, but things always went like this for him. Never picture perfect. He always had to take this call to wait for the picture perfect dream or had to compromise. Why was it supposed to be like this way? Why do other people get an easy and clear verdict? He blamed himself.

He was not sure if he had lost the battle. But the funny thing was he was not sure if he had won it as well.

Anxiety started building up. He felt nauseating with anxiety. He had to make a call. He had to press the 'yes' or 'no' button. But he was afraid if his choice would turn out to be his biggest mistake ever made. Fear and anxiety affected him. He became irritable with people who mattered to him. He felt jealous of people who had a clear choice. He looked up for support. He felt alone insecure and timid.

*That's life.*

*Our choices and decisions govern who we end up becoming.*

□

## Taking the 'Call'

Many people talk about leadership qualities and CEO traits, but I feel the most important thing in a 'leader' is taking the right 'call'. There are organizations in India both government and private sector where no one seems to decide, they just pass the files and avoid taking decision. It is a personality trait which I call 'ball' passing. The reason behind this is probably trying to share responsibility. If you pass the file 15 times, at least 15 people will share the responsibility of the final decision but my question is "will it remain relevant all the time?" There will be times when passing the ball finally is not going to be the option and you will have to take the stand. Great people and great organizations decide and take the 'call'. Leaders stand out from others for somehow they are able to decide on blurred picture and they are ready to put their neck out for the consequences. It may work or may prove wrong, agreed but at least things move forward. This is my firm belief if people learn to 'take call'; they evolve in personal relationships as well. When you are child you can get away with people deciding on your behalf but when you grow up, decision making starts. Just remember – postponing will not kill the problem, facing it will.

□

# TIME MANAGEMENT

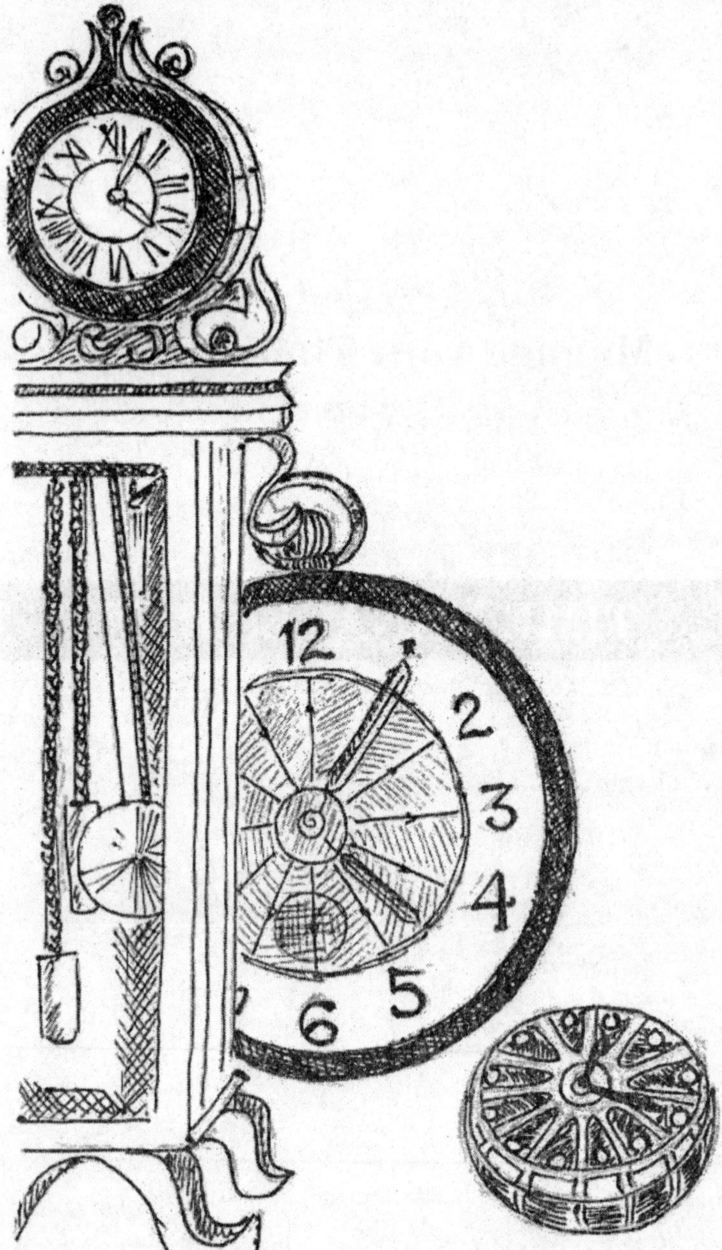

# Manage Your Time Better: Identify the Spurts

**Background:** In my school days, I used to read in books that **slow and steady wins the race**. All great men seemed to be steady workers who would do a little bit every day. You have to be steady and move forward everyday seemed to be the mantra.

**My Reality:** I could never be that steady. I used to think I am doomed. There were days when I didn't feel like working and my output was negligible. I used to think all the future successful people must be working and steadily delivering out their best. But then there were days when I was at my optimum and would be finishing pending tasks.

**Lesson Learnt**: These are days which I now call as my 'Work Spurt' days. Gradually, I learnt to identify these days. Once I feel that I am on roll today, I start taking up more and more challenges and start identifying my pending works. Coffee or tea helps on these days. My method of work is pushing harder on the "work spurt" days and taking it easy on days on the "sloppy days". It was not steady every day but the net result was a upward curve.

*There were plateaus in this graph but there were steep upward lines in between which pushed the graph upward and compensated for plateaus.*

*Manage your time better: identify the Spurts and push the pedal.*

□

## Value Your Own Time

*'Time' is the most valuable asset we all have. Why waste it by reacting to other's actions?*

This is something that I keep telling myself. Often while driving down the Delhi city, I notice people fighting their heart out over small scratch on their cars. On the other hand, if someone by mistake hits my car, I remind myself that people are more important than things and I just raise my hand to show my displeasure and I drive on. As I believe my time in life is better spent constructively rather than reacting it with anger.

That has been the guiding principle of my life, instead of reacting to people, I prefer doing what I want to do.

*Life is too short and time is too less and just too precious to waste it reacting to others.*

□

## Paradox of "Too much to Do, too Little Time"

People keep complaining about lack of time and keep saying they are busy. At times I have seen people who say they are too busy to even talk on phone.

*Well my dear friends it is never about time, it is always about priorities.*

**If you really want to do something you will somehow manage time for they say "where there's a will, there's a way."**

We all have 'less and more time' with us all the time and we keep swinging between the two sides depending upon on our priorities. Why is this so important to know, because you might be spending your precious "time" on things which don't value and if you don't prioritise, you will end up being busy with very little net output. This is what happens in exams, relationships, family and at work.

Many people ask me how I manage my time, the answer is simple, I always work towards my broader instinct, gut feeling and keep checking myself about what I am doing, is it in coherence with broad philosophy of my work. It is so easy to be attracted to more and more and new things, new ventures, but I check them out and choose only those which fit in my 'priority list' and once I want to do something, I don't procrastinate, I just do it right there and then.

Every once in while I meet people who reason out their failure because of lack of time which makes me think, are they missing out on one of the most important assets that is management skill; time management. Mantra for time management is simple – Understand what you want to do, prioritize, make decisions, and don't procrastinate.

***Procrastination makes easy things appear harder and impossible.***

Learn the value of moment and seize your opportunity. Just go ahead and build your career, your dreams. All of us have got 24 hrs/day and each day, each moment has infinite potential provided you prioritize and do what you really want to do, you really need to do; that is the reason why some people are able to take out more out of their '24 hours'.

□

## Sand in Your Hand

Life is like (holding) sand in your hand, you feel you own it and you feel you have control of it but it always manages to slip through your fingers. Time behaves in the same way, you feel you have indefinite time in life, but wise men will say 'time' is the most precious asset you can ever have. Like sand in the hand; time slips, time passes and time flies. If you realize that the time is running out all the time, **would you do the same things over and again, and pursue the same needs. Would you postpone your dreams for later on and would you postpone 'life'?**

□

# THINKING OUT OF THE BOX

# Something Should be Done, At Least They are Doing Something

**Warning:** This would sound outrageous to the few people who always believe that whatever is being done is good for us and for those who actually never think twice about obeying a ritual enforced by any authority.

**Background:** I drove into a shopping mall and a security guard inspected the under surface of my car using a mirror and looked at something as a customary routine activity and then asked me to carry on. I pulled down my window and asked him, "that what did he look for" and the "poor soul" had no idea and said; I was just doing my duty. Then, he said apologetically, just doing what my boss had asked me to and at that moment person sitting by my side interrupted me and said at least they were doing something.

*That was my tipping point, I see this happening everywhere, and we have problems, a lot of them everywhere anywhere. Some of them are personal, some related to organization, some social and some of national and international interest. And someone somewhere in position of power/decision making, when faced with the situation decides something should be done about it. And then solving the problem usually becomes a tough task and people usually succumb to doing something for the sake of doing. They create a ritual. That never ever solves the problem. That ritual was never supposed to work. But when it doesn't work, instead of solving the problem, the team leader, looks to do something, in his view at least something needs to be done, and add another 'namesake' ritual.*

**Question:** I feel everyone should internally audit themselves, find a difference between "rituals" for namesake and 'solutions'. Eliminate namesake rituals, and sweat for solutions. We need solution providers; they might take the longer, harder route but will actually solve the problem.

□

# Sceptic, with a Bit of Faith

Too much faith on everything that is being told to you stalls progress. World moves forward because the sceptics disagree. They don't believe the textbooks and create new paths when there were none. They change the way we understand the world. Most of what we learn in school textbooks has already been proved otherwise in the real world, and most of us didn't even doubt the truth of the textbook.

*Albert Einstein once said, "Blind belief in authority is the greatest enemy of truth."*

But there is another side to it; sometimes sceptics have too many doubts to move forward. They keep doubting and remain in "doubt", while in a team, you need to have faith on leader and his leadership. You need to believe in the concept. People who find it easy to have faith, who actually race to trust, have the advantage of speed. They are able to move forward on faith even before there are evident facts for the 'sceptic' to agree on. They already are deep into it. They get the advantage of time.

*King Martin Luther said, "Faith is taking the first step even when you don't see the whole staircase."*

*Ideal mix for a successful person would be little scepticism, with little bit of faith. He treats new and unknown information with scepticism and the known one with faith.*

*Sceptic for the what he hears as facts from books, media and newspapers and chooses "the faith" way for the people close to him.*

□

## Knowledge on the Edge

There are things which are unknown to the vast majority of people. They may have to do with history, what exactly happened in past, they may have to do with future; science or industry. There are things which most of us don't have an access to. But few on edge always know and decide what 'we' should know and what is not good for 'us' to know.

Problem is not with their knowing or not knowing, problem is always with a select few deciding what goes into public domain or not.

*Haven't we all felt at times, that we don't know exactly hat happened in the past? Are the history textbooks really factual?*

*Haven't we all at times suspected the food that we eat, air that we breathe and medicines that we use? What if someone somewhere knows what is wrong with them and chooses not to share.*

And sometime in future when this fringe knowledge becomes mainstream, it will be a revolutionary break through. There are always people who were privy to this information even before that.

*Where is the future located?*

*It is already located on fringes of today.*

□

## Winds of Change

Things change, people change and the way things are done is changing faster than ever before.

There is a risk for everybody in whatever he/she is doing. That risk is to be outdated. You need to adapt fast, probably learn everything on the way and run. If you are happy with status quo it is highly likely that you are already outdated.

Most important skill for anyone today is not pure talent, that won't take you far. Most important skill is adaptability to change.

*Let me quote Darwin here, "It is not the strongest of the species that survive, nor the most intelligent, but the one most responsive to change."*

□

## Look Beyond Self-Imposed Boundaries

We all end up living a life given to us by circumstances and most of us draw a boundary to our "world". We don't see the entire world, we don't experience vastness of the world, we just remain closed in our circumscribed, tunnel. Some people call it "living in your comfort zone". We preserve our ego by limiting our self to small space around us.

*Step 1 towards understanding your own self is to widen your horizon. Notice more things than you normally do. Do look up and out from your mobile device there is a beautiful world out there....*

□

# Ultrasound in the Shopping Centre

Other day I was walking in the shopping complex in Delhi, I could see many people in gym attire and I realized that there is a popular gym in shopping mall. You name a thing and you will find it in the mall. Many people nowadays spend significant time in shopping complexes, will it have some implications for ultrasounds especially for pregnant ladies. I am sure many of them would be visiting the mall like others and would love to get a souvenir clicked by the sonographer, preferably 3D image. That image can be framed by the vendor and would be a good remembrance for the parents. However, jokes apart, one of the major factors this will not happen in India in near future is the PNDT Act prohibiting such a usage.

For the conventional thinkers, I do agree that this can never be for medical purposes, this cannot be considered a medically sound advice, but with the amount of time affluent people spend in shopping complexes, some of private healthcare providers will gradually find their way in. Skin care and cosmetics have valid reasons to be there. I foresee corporate health check up being offered in a shopping mall rather than the hospital. They will have much more walk in clients as compared to hospitals. It is so difficult to motivate someone healthy to visit the hospital.

*Future doesn't always take the predictable route. And history has often revealed markets shift to where consumers are. Google and Facebook are classical examples.*

□

## Lateral Thinking

By lateral thinking I mean, Whenever I am travelling, most of the domestic airlines I see them selling trashy products and hardly anyone is interested in buying them. One day I asked the crew that why didn't they provide any newspaper on flight (low cost airlines)? if instead of carrying the load of these products (which hardly sell) you could just sell newspapers at the beginning of flight at say ₹ 20, 50 or even 100 almost everyone on board will buy one as we have almost nothing to do for the journey, you add value to our journey and your airlines ends up making more money (imagine selling at 25 times the cost price). May be someone started selling trashy products on board and everyone else is just following the course without thinking.

*Lateral thinking is a phrase often used but seldom understood; there are always simpler or better ways of doing a thing, which we are unable to see as we are strongly biased by the status quo.*

*My two cents on life and work, just because something is being done in one particular way for long time doesn't exactly mean that it is the best solution.*

□

## Learn to Unlearn

Most people once they taste success, form habits and prejudice about how things work. But somehow that initial magic is not recreated again and again. Let me share a secret here: people win because they take initial good decisions based on instinct at the right time while they end up giving credit to their plans and calculations. That is where they become one time wonders. If you can 'learn to unlearn' the extensive surveys and pros and cons analysis, and learn to go by your gut feeling, your instinct, you will know that you always knew what is to be done next. Every time I postpone things for analysis later on, even at the moment of delaying decision making, something inside me knows what should be done and that is what I ultimately end up doing. That is the power of instinct and I sincerely feel if you 'learn to unlearn' the extra baggage and trust your instinct, you move up the ladder faster and higher.

□

# Planning Versus Intuitiveness

All along my life, I have met people who have plans for years ahead, who have five-year and ten-year goals and then there were people with not too many plans, just some ideas and willingness to play. If planning and crystal balling was everything, then those people should have really done well while in reality all they could plan was their next job, next promotion and so on. Planners never actually touch lives, which is my definition of success. To me key to success in life is being intuitive (like your mothers know you're lying). Same is said about software or mobile phones having *intuitive* interface. Some people attribute their intuition to the power of subconscious or just an act of faith. To me ability to know the unknown without actually going into the micro details, ability to visualize the bigger picture even when the things are foggy is the key to success. It is good to know that people plan for best schools, colleges, and hope that their plans would make them or their children successful, but success, the haughty lady, prefers to go the few who are intuitive, non-conformist men who actually outrun plans by intuition. World is dynamic and it is always looking for favourable mutants as goes the age-old Charles Darwin's words "survival of the fittest". This cannot be done by planning; it can only be done by intuition. This is the way of nature, and nature looks for non-conformists who survive the environmental changes and that's how Darwinian evolution also took place. Many people ask me how I planned my work, while I actually never planned anything, just went with the flow.

*Let's not play to fit in, let's play to be our true selves. Do what you actually believe, follow your heart, your gut feeling...flow like a river who just knows where to go....*

□

# Intellectual Cowardice

This strange topic is centre point of how successful you are likely to get in life, both in material and non-material sense. There are people who exhibit a strange kind of fear or paranoid feeling when confronted with an intellectually challenging situation, and instead of getting into a healthy debate, they usually pack off and escape. The questions might relate to way things are done in the organization, or may be related to their faith or their beliefs. Some people are afraid to discuss, and they just blurt out that they know it all and there is no point in discussing any further. The term that is used for such a behaviour is intellectual cowardice. This implies and includes: the fear to question, the fear to use intelligence when confronted with a defying question which challenges the way you have been doing things so far, and questions regarding your strategy of life which seem to be working for you so far. These people either back off from such questions or resort to aggression. And that's where the progress stops. This is a sign of mental orthodox and complacent behaviour. If you are able to take challenging questions with intelligent thought process and are able to modify your own set of beliefs based on logical reasoning, you evolve and proceed to the next level. Most successful people are those who have courage to raise questions and more importantly courage to face questions regarding their own selves. These are people who help the organizations and process evolve by challenging and in turn promoting a culture of questioning from time to time, which is so vital for a personality or an organization to grow.

If everything that you know was perfect and unquestionable, then why does science keep surprising us with new discoveries, why do people keep finding new ways to make profitable enterprises if all options are already exhausted? Let's all be aware of this sin called as intellectual cowardice, and avoid it by being open to questions which challenge our beliefs and see the things as they are, not as they are presented to us, let's not become so rigid that even sound advice doesn't bend us. According to a famous Talmud quote: "We do not see things as they are, we see them as we are."

And I believe people with intellectual courage challenge notions and perceptions while people with cowardice become cynical.

□

## Taj Mahal Seekers

The title of this article is little confusing and actually I am not talking about 'Taj Mahal' per se but I am using it as a symbol of beautiful and perfect end-product. Are you one of those who believe in creating your Taj Mahal first and then selling it? Is this what your school teacher taught you? I simply don't agree. Idea of success in life, business and exams is to know right time to act and to be able to make quick decisions. I know of people who wait till they achieve perfection to actually launch the product into market and realise that the idea doesn't sell. Taj Mahal is good to see; people will say wow but may not buy an apartment in it. Idea is to know when your product is workable and be able to bring it to market before others do. I had colleagues in school and college who in search of perfection wasted too much time in reading too much material and always scored lower than me in exams, while my idea was somehow to make a right mix which could be done fast enough to hit the exam deadlines. Usually, my idea is to work towards Taj Mahal and not wait till perfection for launching. Something that ails us as a nation as well is lack of speed in implementation and may be the ministers studied in the same Taj Mahal school and are waiting for the perfect plan. Problem is by the time the decision is made and the 'perfect' plan is implemented, the product no longer remains relevant in most cases and someone else has already become the first mover. Learn to anticipate, think fast and don't be afraid to hit the market with a ready but not perfect product as goes my mantra for success.

□

# Fringe Vision

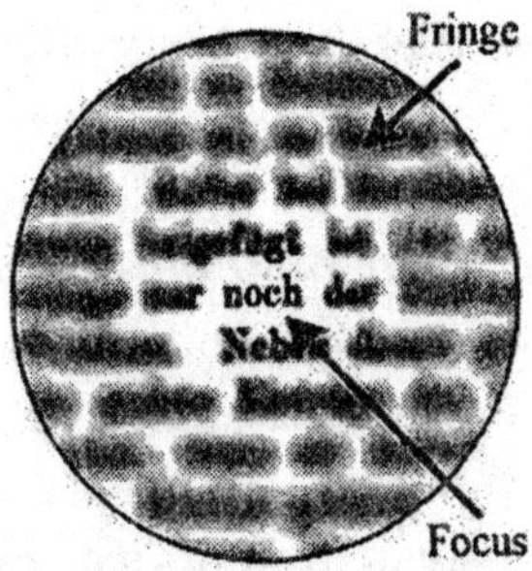


There are two ways to lead your life, one is to stay focused on what you are doing and have a tunnelled vision with your definition of the world being 'you' and "people connected to you". Do you actually notice things around and see what is happening? I am sure many people reading this would say what is wrong in this and would claim to notice everything.

*My question here is: What is it that scientists, artists, winners do differently to achieve extraordinary success?*

Again, some of you would claim yourself to be successful in your own way, agreed, but here I am talking of extraordinary success, something which is phenomenal, which changes the way people think and do things.

I am talking of the kind of work artists and scientists do. Here is my take on it; these are people who are more alert to what is happening in the fringe of their visual field. They notice things which normal people don't notice. Artists would notice them and paint the picture with details which surprises the viewers; photographers freeze moments which we just passed by without noticing. Poets find pain in what is happening around them and we just pass by. True scientists would notice things in their peripheral vision, sometimes what was obviously seen, but was being missed by everybody, is noticed by someone and science progresses. History is full of such examples where the obvious was being missed, for example something like Newton's discovery of gravity, and now we take it for granted. Somehow, I feel, this is what medicine books also try to teach us. Notice the patient as a whole, then zero down on field of interest, and radiology is similar, take an overview, and then focus on pathology. Good students notice things in the fringe and answer even the rare questions in exam and get more marks. Great physicians notice things which others missed and treat the patient in one brilliant moment.

Developing fringe vision is one art which I feel is being missed, probably for a simple reason, that it gets overwhelming to notice everything and feel pain of everything, probably the over curious and sensitive people are more alert to the fringes and their work brings the fringe to the visual field of the mainstream.

□

# Let's not Kill the Innovation and Scepticism

Who are the people who make difference to this world? Do you think people who are ok with what is happening, who believe everything told (or fed) to them and take it as truth; are the ones? I would place my bet on the other kind, the odd sceptic, one who beg to differ and want to ask the question. Who disagrees with the norm and seeks reason before making his opinion. I believe we need thick skinned innovators and curious people in all streams to answer more questions. If we look back in history every discovery, every big idea and every big business was somewhere built out of someone's desire to not to agree to what is being taken as truth or norm. I have a feeling our education system somewhere rewards the "straight line fellows" and kind of snubs the sceptics/questioning people. There ought to be revolutionary change in education system which respects people with questioning mind because they will make the future different from present and bring new revolutionary answers. In my own experience, when we added Sky (Satellite)-based initiative to our classroom network in DAMS, some people were sceptical, they said video conferencing doesn't work and now with 50-plus centres already it has brought classes to places where such facilities were unheard of.

Let's not pause here, there is no final answer, there is no perfect truth, therefore keep the curiosity alive. Things which were thought as impossible once upon a time are now day-to-day use items. They came into existence because someone questioned and someone was not happy with status quo.

□

## Flexibility-Identify the 'Nudges'

Whenever we start our journey for creating a valuable enterprise, some of us end up creating something wonderful and some of us don't. To me one of the most important difference between people who create value is flexibility.

Recounting my own experience, whenever, I have started a new segment in my company, I have always started with a broad/blurred vision and then gradually worked on microscopic details. And often end-product was not what I had or could have imagined in the beginning. Some of us make the mistake of visualizing the end-product too soon and become the prisoner of our own prejudice.

Path to success is not a rigid path, on the way you get **soft nudges** guiding you to your path of glory, but if you are too rigid, you may not benefit from them. Nudges may come from your employees, your consumers, social media inputs or even a family member. Sometimes things which are plainly obvious to people around the entrepreneur, may be hitting his blind spot. So the golden rule is to start with broad plan of action, be receptive to people around you, encourage a culture of transparency, identify the valuable **'signs'** or **'soft nudges'** gentling sculpturing your initial thought/idea into a beautiful end product.

□

# Innovation: The How and Why of It

*We all have heard this before. There is a need for innovative answers to difficult solutions that we face in day to day life/business. But how do we go about it?*

Here is four-point plan for being a successful innovator.

**Be curious:** Curiosity is one of the most important qualities required for success and is not given its correct due in most of the schools in India where people who can follow the routine are favoured. Let's be curious and ask questions, you will find surprising answers in everything you thought was so routine, so obvious.

**Look at problems as opportunities:** Major difference between innovators and other people is the way they look at problems. Innovators look at problem as a chance to create an extraordinary solution to the problem. Innovators love to break through road blocks to find out of the box solutions.

**Be frugal:** There is a difference in innovation done by larger corporations and individuals. Particularly in developing nations we should look at the cost of R&D and value generated. Go for *alternatives* (colloquially as we say *jugaad*), and create low cost solutions to big problems.

**Generate value:** Innovation should serve a purpose, and widen the usage, making a large impact on the end users. It should fill the gap.

□

# Extrapolation

Mathematically, extrapolation is a way to make guess about some hypothetical situation based on data that you already know.

*For example, read this line: he stepped out of his black BMW.*

*You extrapolated him to be a rich man.*

*But, in fact, he was working as a driver in a big company.*

That is exactly what happens in an exam or share market or relationship for that matter.

We all extrapolate based on our experience on the subject concerned. When faced with a new decision (which we don't know) mind extrapolates from what we know to what could be the answer to current problem. People with gaps in their knowledge and training are likely to extrapolate to wrong conclusions.

That is the role of experience and training you learn to 'extrapolate' correctly.

*Try this question now:*

*Light bulb sign on x-ray is seen in-posterior dislocation of shoulder.*

*Now, if you do only so-called MCQ guide books and have not studied the concept.*

*Imagine getting a question in exam: Which shoulder dislocation is easier to identify on x-ray?*

*Pause*

*Your mind is likely to extrapolate to posterior while the answer is anterior. Posterior dislocation is actually tough to identify.*

That's the risk of fragmented knowledge.

Extrapolation is an inherent human trait. Our subconscious works faster than conscious and uses extrapolation to solve things that we don't know.

*Winners extrapolate correctly and others make blunders.*

□

## Limited by Thought

Where do we reach in life is often not limited by talent but by our ability to think and visualise. How will you feel, if you get to know that you yourself are the real limiting factor to your own growth. Often good people, talented ones, don't reach to the levels we think they would, simply because of lack of vision.

You can see only up to a certain distance in the time zone and thereafter it becomes blurred and uncertain.

Leaders see things "beyond the visible" and in no course of time when they bring that into the zone of reality and present, surprising everyone.

To avoid being limited by your thought, you need to broaden your horizon. Essential tools for this skill are probably reading, travelling and strong sense of intuition. An open receptive mind does matter to. Listen to others, may be they can help you see what you couldn't see yourself.

*As Bruce Lee once said, "As you think, so shall you become."*

□

## Little Bit of Madness

**Normal People:** Life is predictable. They like conforming to the norm. Norm is defined by the society in general. They hate change. They cannot stand people who are different. They want to be safe all the time.

**Mad Ones:** They perceive and see the world different from the "normal" ones. Some of them see colours in a different way and become painters. Some of them hear music in places where others hear noise and they become musicians. They hate to conform. Normal people hate them. They are never safe.

*Some of them are so mad that they lose total touch with reality but some of them have with them just a little bit madness, just enough to create, to make a difference and to bring the change.*

As rightly said by **Friedrich Nietzsche.**

*"And those who were seen dancing were thought to be insane by those who could not hear the music."*

□

## Afraid to Think Different, Are You?

*You are used to living and thinking in a certain way. And you assume it to be the only and the only version of truth. Your survival as 'you' and your entire 'belief' set is based on this thinking process. As soon as someone suggests something different, you get uncomfortable. You disagree and at times you even get angry. You fight in the name of belief. You are not ready to even listen to it. You cannot be wrong after all these years of believing something.*

*Are you afraid to even entertain a 'thought' different from your 'belief'?*

This is what I do, when I encounter a thought, which is diametrically opposite to my "belief set"; I let the initial phase of disagreement and anger pass. Then, I allow the thought to settle in my mind and understand the view point of the other side. Then, I choose to agree or disagree. I feel this is how; you should expand your thought process and evolve as a person.

*Think about it.*

*Are you even afraid to think 'different'?*

☐

# WORK AND LIFE

## Time Flies

There he was, walking towards the gate of building. It usually took him five-minutes to reach till the gate.

Today something was different. It was taking him longer than usual. He was short of breath. The door seemed so far away. He thought to himself, was this it?

It was happening so abruptly. He never thought the end would be so abrupt. He always thought it would be like changing a job, he always thought he would get time to say good bye to all, finish his pending desires. Yes, there were so many things left undone, so many words still to be said.

*But yes, time flies.*

Make sure you say what you really want to say, while you can.

Make sure, you follow your heart, your dreams your aspirations; not people's perspective of what you should be.

Make sure you live while you still can.

*For, Time flies.*

□

## Timeless Moments

Time moves at different speeds at different points in our life.

There are moments which appear to drag. These moments are usually 'sad' or 'stressful' moments which don't seem to end.

Then, there are moments which just fly away. These are usually 'happy' or 'winning' moments. They always seem to end just too fast.

And then there are some 'timeless' moments when time doesn't matter. Those are the moments which make our lives worthwhile. Those are moments which we cherish and fill up our memory as still images. These are moments when we stop counting and start living.

*As Albert Einstein said, "Time is just an illusion."*

□

## Real Stories have No Conclusions

As a child we are taught a story with a definitive structure comprising of beginning, a middle part and an ending. Then, when we grow up, we start looking for conclusions in life as well. We always want results just as stories have conclusions. We keep asking for an ending.

When we find conclusions elusive, we start getting restless. Life doesn't seem to go like a movie.

*Because life is journey not a destination.*

You win every moment, you lose every moment. You start living when you stop looking for conclusions.

*Just as a master story teller leaves the ending open for the reader to conjure, real life also does not have conclusions.*

□

## What If?

He had a busy life. Never really had the time to think about anything else than work. He had just boarded his flight to reach to next destination for an important assignment. As soon as the flight attendants announced, He stood up to take out his laptop and started making his next presentation. Side by side, he was answering pending emails. He had all the time in life to do what he wanted to. He wanted to conquer the world and be at top.

Then, suddenly plane started to quiver, bad weather, he mumbled without even looking up. Then, it became more and more shaky. People started to shout.

*He looked around, he thought was this it? What about all the things he had wanted to do in this life? Things he had been postponing. Everything he was doing seemed to be futile and in vain. He wanted another chance. He wanted another 'START' full of regret and remorse he felt his life was waste.*

Captain's voice broke his chain of thoughts. Plane was in control now. He was alive and back to work again. He looked around. People around him were "unknowns". Talking, eating and creating a familiar irritating noise.

*Then, he thought to himself, "What should be the background colour for the next slide on his PowerPoint presentation....*

□

# Keeping Pace with Life

At times life seems to move faster than life itself. In order to take more out of your day, you shift to faster cars and chose best possible flights to get more out of the day. When you are rushing through, you just are focussed on targets and speed. Targets keep getting tougher and speed is never fast enough.

One day I decided to make it point to go slow. I deliberately took a wrong turn and felt the joy of having taken **'ROAD NOT TAKEN'** without knowing where it would lead. I had to keep an eye on surroundings to trace the path back towards my destination. I noticed more than usual as my awareness was awakened by the anxiety of travelling on new path.

I noticed there were so many things and people on my way which didn't exist for me so far. I saw the red flowers on the trees and people on the road. I saw the florist around the corner and river on the way. I noticed a group of beggar children on the traffic light. I saw their faces and eyes. They were real people. They had stories and aspiration similar to ones we have after all they were real people.

*When we rush, life shows you blurred surroundings. But when we slow down a bit, blur clears and reality reveals.*

□

# Postponing Life

He lived his life for a better tomorrow. He said he will work now and live tomorrow. Compromise today and dreams will be taken care of tomorrow as was his belief. He started this in school when teachers told him; work today and live tomorrow. He worked and he slogged. He longed for tomorrow. His heart wanted to follow his dreams, but people told him, dreams can wait, let the routine prevail for today.

*Question remains, my friends: What if tomorrow never comes? And so does the Hindi quote:*

*Kaal Kare So Aaj Kar, Aaj Kare So Ub*
*Pal Mein Pralaya Hoyegi, Bahuri Karoge Kub*

काल करे सो आज कर, आज करे सो अब
पल में परलय होएगी बहूरी करोगे कब।

*Translation*

Tomorrow's work do today, today's work now. If the moment is lost, the work be done how.

□

## Chase

Charm of life is in the chase. To chase is one of our natural instincts. When you want something elusive, all your senses are focussed on achieving it and distractions don't seem to matter. You feel the need to reach to your destination; you feel the thrill of the chase. And when you reach your target, although you have won, you miss the adrenaline surge you had all the way along the chase, you miss the thrill of chase and then you seek another challenge.

*As they say, "it is always the journey which is more enticing than the destination."*

□

## Ephemeral Kingdom

Word 'ephemeral' means "things that last for a very short time." They imply things are which transitory in nature. Somehow, this is the best phrase that I could write to explain what we do in life without actually thinking over it, is just ephemeral.

Many kings were busy building castles and palaces. Acquisition of new pieces of land and gold kept them busy. Similar to many of us for we spend most of our time building ephemeral kingdoms, just like the kings of the past.

*Neither their kingdoms did not last and nor will ours.*

*Question that we should ask ourselves every day, "are we postponing what really matters to us for an uncertain tomorrow in lieu of creating our so-called kingdom."*

□

# Destiny

His inner voice told him to take an off that day. He was not feeling good about the day, may be it was because of weather. It had been raining all week. It was dark, wet, and gloomy.

Still he ignored the feeling, and went ahead to work.

People on the road looked strangely aloof to him.

He saw the red light in front of him. He knew in this weather he needs to be careful. But somehow he ignored his inner self and jumped the light. He kept driving with limited visibility. He thought he should be on the side and wait for the visibility to improve. Yet, he moved on. May be work in office was important. He had never missed work for such a petty reason.

Suddenly, he heard a loud sound. And then he felt his head striking the steering. And last thought that came to his mind was he should have stayed at home.

*He always knew something was wrong.*

*Somehow we always know.... Yet sometimes destiny takes the lead over our good sense.*

□

## Wings of Freedom

### Prologue

*Just like us he was another common man, busy in work and family. He was taught to be the best in everything he did; he was always building something, home for family, office for work and relationships. Every second of his life was precious. He believed in optimum utilization of his time and resources. For he believed "Time was money". He had good connections with everyone. Email and Facebook were one of the few things that he checked first in the morning. He loved to party. He loved to celebrate every moment. There was noise on road and hustle bustle all around.*

*The moment things got silent he would pick up his phone and call someone.*

*That was life, busy, connected, constructive and noisy.*

*One day it all ended. Everything had come to an end. He died.*

### He was a bird now:

Wait a minute, he was no more yet he could feel he was still there, his body felt strange. He was small; reincarnated as a bird. But the strange thing was he could still think like a human. Being the world's first intelligent bird.

## Silence:

He started to fly around, first thing he noticed was silence, and he wanted his mobile phone. High above the sky, there was silence and there was no Facebook to update his status. He suffered just like an addicted suffers from withdrawal. He wanted to shout. Days passed and he could gradually hear his own voice, he was coming back from his only 'human' days. He met his own self for the first time amidst the silence of the clouds.

## Time-less (free from time):

He wanted to know what time of the day it was. He searched for the clock tower, all of a sudden then he realized that it is only humans who have made the clock tower. So obsessed he got with time, that he decided to stay near the clock tower. Days and months passed together and he got used to it and as a result time didn't matter anymore. He was free. He was no more time bound.

## Want to build my home and save for future:

Like the rest as all humans do, he wanted a home, that he could call his own. He was always collecting stuff to decorate. While all others were flying free. He was always collecting stuff and food for future. He made a small collection of food items which he would use in times of emergency. This was his insurance. Then one day he stopped because....

## Faith:

He realized he could fly high in sky like birds because they have faith. They can hear and enjoy their own voice. He could fly because he had the power of faith and courage and now he knew that he won't fall. He need not collect anymore because there is plenty for everyone in nature. And if you enjoy the flight the time doesn't matter anymore.

**Free at last:**

Finally, he was free. From time, noise, THE need to collect and with faith on his wings he could fly free. He was a free bird.

□

## Are We Becoming a 'Jerkistan'

What is wrong with people in our country, have we all lost sensibility and sensitivity? You move out of your house and you meet fools after fools. First one would have parked his car in front of yours and would have gone somewhere, after you successfully find him, and move ahead another one would cross you from wrong side and a fool driving a bus would act as if he is driving a motorcycle and would go zig-zag on the road being ignorant about others' life on the road. By the time you get over them another 'ONE' would be honking non-stop and another 'ONE' in front of you would be talking on phone and his car would be standing motion less in front of you. All of a sudden you would hear an ambulance siren asking for the way and fools ahead wouldn't seem to listen. You would see an old lady waiting to cross the road and these fools would just ignore her. You board a bus, a fool would be sitting on the seat listening to music with his headphones on and an old uncle would be standing by the side. People eat half of the food that they order and throw the other half and wouldn't be ready to give it the "poor" who helps them day and night. You will notice that there are ones who think that is their birth right to stare at women walking by and passing a comment would make them look smart. They will break the queues, go from the wrong side and cause a jam. They will play loud music because they are having a party with little regard for others, block roads because they are having a social event while others will get stuck and they would be least bothered. Somehow, as a common man I feel, we all know the rules, we are argumentative, we are competitive but all that we need to acquire is sensitivity and basic respect for humans in general and in no time we will be able to build a better place better nation for everyone around. Patience and respect for co-existent human beings is grossly missing, and trust me this is not about the government, it is about us.

□

# Virtual Relationships

This is a story about 2025.

Facebook and social media have extensively evolved and offer a variety of new features like auto updating of status from news about your favourite topics, thanking people for liking updates, responding to comments, viz., automatic smiley icons. With a bit of artificial intelligence coming into picture now there are pre-drafted intelligent replies to mails sent to you, not just the **'run of the mill'** message available now. These automatic replies will be pertinent to the subject and will appear as if they have been drafted by the person sending them. After one point of time people would have achieved immortality at least on social media (Facebook). You will continue to be alive on Facebook even after you are gone, with automatic updates and comments.

But the ironic part is, "people who don't matter (to you) and are (just) friends on Facebook, will not know the difference at all."

□

## Stuck in the City of Dreams

Many people come to the city Delhi for instance, from far and near with dreams and aspirations. In each city, there are clusters of people having different type of aspirations. These clusters have constantly evolving populations. Handful of them reach their dream destinations, achieve spectacular success and their stories encourage many other to come to the city in pursuit of their dreams.

Then, there are some who give up and go back to their origin and forgo their dreams.

Some of them compromise and accept the opportunities that come their way as God's will and forgo their original dream and someone of them get stuck. Yes, some of them do get stuck. You see them on traffic lights, footpaths everywhere anywhere looking here and there with sense of hopelessness and helplessness.

*You see them for a moment; pretend to think about for you actually don't think much about what must have happened and then race on to your pursuit.*

□

# Age Thermostat

They were there on the airport. Father was white haired, spectacled man, unsure of the place. By the way he was going about it you could easily make out, he was not a frequent flyer to say the least. He went into the security check with his cell phone in his tunic's (kurta's) pocket. The young security personal got restless and sent him back to put the cell phone in the tray to be passed for scanning under x-ray. Someone else had moved forward by this time. Old man not sure of himself, decided to stand in the queue again.

At last everyone got through!!

His son young man, clean shaven, stocky built was restlessly waving at his father. He asked him, why did he take this long? Father looked at him apologetically. Son along with some authority guided him towards the boarding gate. All the time, you could hear him describe the airport with a confidence of a frequent flyer.

*Everyone grows old. Everyone is a small weepy kid at one point of time. Then, why don't people show the obvious desired warmth to extremes of age. Probably, defect lies in our age thermostat. Our definition of young and old is different for ourselves and others. Our mind preserves a young image of ourselves and presents a favourable image of our own-self and hence you see people as older and don't ever see yourself reaching that point.*

□

## Put *Your Feet* in *My Shoes*, and See What it is Like

We live in a strongly opinionated dogmatic society full of preconceived ideas. We take no time to form opinions about what is right, and what is not. We 'apparently' happen to know exactly what everyone else is supposed to do. All this is possible because we assume that other person will behave in a particular fashion for instance as any machine does. There are standards to be followed rules to be adhered to and conditions to be kept in mind. Surprisingly, we are more lenient with ourselves and expect higher standards from others. We all have opinions on how some celebrity should behave and how the country should be run.

*One thing I feel that should be introduced in all education systems is role playing.*

For example, I learnt more about the hospital when I first went with a family member from my better half's side. It changed my perspective altogether. I learnt faster than my years in the classroom as a medical student.

Be a leader of your class for a few weeks and you will understand why leading a country might be humungous task. (I realised this when I was the president in my residency days.) Lesson that I learnt as the college president was that you cannot please everyone and anyone 'you want' to and taking a stand is what a leader needs to do. I could not have learnt this by watching leaders on TV or reading in the books.

*Probably that is the reason people who have been on both the sides understand the others' perspective better.*

*Imagine an education system which allows "you to be someone else sometime."*

Imagine a system where doctors in training spend time in formative years in patient's waiting rooms. Be at the reception desk of a busy bank or airport for a day before shouting at someone for being lazy next time. Go without food for a day before criticising someone for begging or stealing for food.

*That would make us more empathic, helping us understand other person's motive and as to what he does.*

*Close your eyes and imagine being in someone else's shoes, before passing the next judgement and world would be a better place.*

Get angry today, regret tomorrow.

Anger kills peace and relationships more than anything else. You always have a choice to speak when you are angry and hurt someone or to stay silent.

I often take route of silence and usually end up realizing that it was not worth losing temper in first place and if I had spoken at that time it would have scarred the relationship for ever. This 'understanding' comes when you understand the joy of present moment.

Next time when someone or something makes you really angry and you get annoyed, stay silent.

It will probably save you from the regret of the lifetime.

□

## Mindless Conversations

People want to stay connected with each other, but I think they have nothing in common with each other. But the need to stay connected is what causes the connection to be built. As time passes by, there is nothing meaningful left to be shared nothing left to be discussed. What is to be done then? Share a joke? Copy and paste from one group to another. I feel it is good to share the laughter once in a while but all the time, do we really need to do it?

*Are we better placed 'NOW' in the hyper-connected world or it was the past that was better when you had lost touch with people or is it still the same.*

*Remember mindless conversations cannot be called being in touch, anyway.*

□

# COMMON SENSE

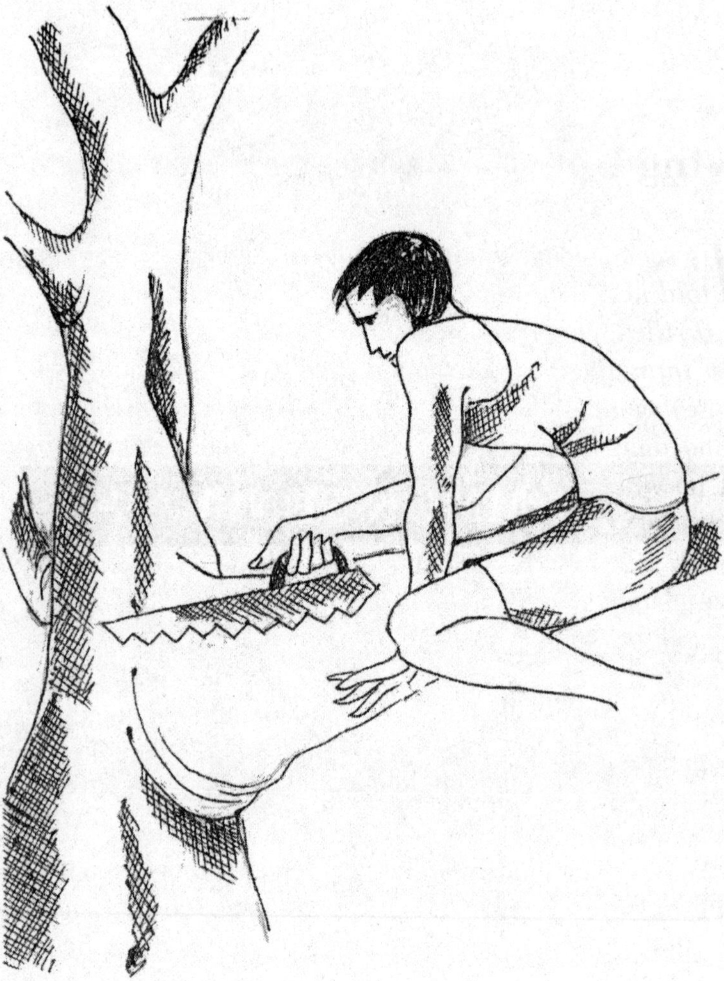

## Living Up to a Mirage of Self-Image

*His school teacher applauded him for his work. She told him that he had an I.Q. more than his age. He was thrilled. It was not routine affair. He had performed better than others he felt and so did the teachers say.*

Few years from now, life was not going like what he had imagined it to be in school. But he still believed that he was extraordinary. This belief of him led to his exaggeration of self-image within himself and forced him to work more than necessary. He was always trying to prove it to himself that his belief was right. Most of his ventures were not successful. He neglected his family and life in to be that extraordinary one. He was intelligent beyond his age; remember this was what the teacher had said. Life was moving faster than he had imagined it to be and he was nothing but just another average man with his ego still hanging on to that superlative image.

*Some of us run away from our life in order to confirm that exaggerated self-image we have created for ourselves and in pursuit of which we forget to value our ordinary, normal world.*

*Yes, ordinary is beautiful.*

□

## Freedom from Being Judged

At times it feels strange that people always opine about you. Even people who hardly know you have strong opinions so as to how you should lead your life.

*They judge each and every move each and every action.*

When things are going in your favour, they will judge you as intelligent, confident and visionary. On the other hand, same set of people when you go wrong will label you as fool, insensible and not so confident person in no time. This time despite being the same you, you get over ambitious, short-sighted and restless for you valued there opinion just too seriously and tune yourself to prove them wrong. It appears as if somehow everyone is aware as to how others are supposed to lead their lives rather than their own.

Subconsciously, we tend to modify our actions to get their approval.

*We stop living and start conforming.*

*Do we ever get freedom from being judged and do we spare others when it is our turn to judge?*

□

# Beware of Chauffeur Knowledge in Medical Education

Here is a famous story eliciting a very important point. After receiving the Nobel Prize in Physics in 1918, Max Planck went on tour across Germany. Wherever he was invited, he delivered the same lecture on new quantum mechanics. Over time, his chauffeur grew to know it by heart: "It has to be boring giving the same speech each time, Professor Planck. How about I do it for you in Munich? You can sit in the front row and wear my chauffeur's cap. That'd give us both a bit of variety." Planck liked the idea, so that evening the driver held a long lecture on quantum mechanics in front of a distinguished audience. Later, a physics professor stood up with a question. The driver recoiled: "Never would I have thought that someone from such an advanced city as Munich would ask such a simple question! My chauffeur will answer it" *(The Art of Thinking Clearly* by Rolf Dobelli*)*.

What does this story teach us, all our lives especially in today's Internet era we are flooded with information. Some people appear fancy, speak well and their Facebook pages have followers. But trust me a chauffeur with a well-rehearsed lecture may appear like Planck, without actually having any inside to it. Medical education especially in India is full of such 'chauffeurs'. Imagine a scenario today where people who have not even done MD medicine, claim to have compiled mistakes in Harrison's textbook. They are chauffers in medicine.

In this world, we have two kinds of knowledge. One is Planck knowledge, the people who really know. They've paid the dues, they have the aptitude. And then we've got chauffeur knowledge.

They have learned the talk. They may have a big head of hair, they may have fine temper in the voice, they'll make a hell of an impression.

But in the end, all they have is chauffeur knowledge. □

## Being Yourself

Are you really comfortable with your own self? When do you think a person is most attractive? My answer is and will be when he is being himself. How many times have we met people who act super smart, super confident, who pretend to know it all and have it all and how many times have we noticed that in the end they are a total put off. Nothing attracts more than authentic nature of person. To be yourself, you need to love yourself, have that self-pride which allows you to be the 'real you' in different situations. Another advantage of being genuine is the fact that you can carry it on for a longer duration. Sometimes, you will notice relationships start on pretence and ultimately you get tired for acting out the role and pretending out that you really are not. Easiest way is be yourself and act like you do and trust me being yourself is effortless. Further, you end up attracting right people towards you, who like you for the right reasons.

*Don't try to be somebody you're not because it doesn't work. Be yourself. Be who you want to be.*

□

## Vision, Common Sense and Criticism

There are three kinds of people:

Category 1: Confused, they cannot see the obvious, they cannot see what is in front of them, they analyse everything with prejudice and bias that they have accumulated in their life all along.

Category 2: One with common sense, they are able to see things like they are. They see and understand without prejudice without bias.

Category 3: Visionaries, they see what other don't. They are like 'THE CRYSTAL BALL' the orbuculum who can predict the future. They are CLAIRVOYANTS they see gold where others see dust.

And 'people with vision' create, people with 'common sense' and people with 'confusions' criticise.

□

## ‘You are Right But...’

If you are one of those, who start of a conversation with,” you are right but...” or “It was good but...” make sure you are aware that this is a classic put off line for any conversation. Either I am right or wrong; this statement which starts with a positive then adds an unnecessary negative line will not take you to places. True leadership is achieved when you learn to appreciate truly without riders and pokes in between.

□

## Art of Listening

There are times when I meet people who speak, speak and only speak. I am sure we have actually gotten phone calls from people who speak and speak and somehow whatever you say hits the wall. There are times when you can make it out and know that this person is not going to get the point you are trying to make just because he didn't learn the art of listening in school. Hearing the other person out is a skill and making mental notes of the conversation helps a lot especially when you are discussing something important. Try this voluntarily if this is not a skill you have been blessed with. Most people over-rate speaking and keep speaking to look smart while on the other speaking exposes their irrational 'unwitty' side. Learn to stay silent, listen to others patiently and you will end up looking the smartest and end up making the most valid points. Same applies for students, some people seem to speak rather than listen and they come to me for counselling and keep telling me, what all they know, and wouldn't allow me to speak. Look at the irony look at the paradox, you go to someone for advice and you don't listen to him at all, you just keep talking without a pause, at times I just go blunt on them by saying if you know it all, why are you not getting the required results. Mostly, I get them to listen to sense and trust me that works wonders. Listening is so common sense and yet good listeners are uncommon. Good listeners actually listen beyond words, read between lines and get the most out of the conversation. Like it is often quoted, “there’s a lot of difference between listening and hearing.” And I feel that somehow makes a huge difference in where you end up finally.

Be Interesting by Becoming Interested. Remember God gave us a mouth that closes and ears that don’t. There is a reason think about it.

□

# How Many Teachers do You Remember in Life?

Teaching as a profession has not got its due place in India. Probably, because most (not all) of our school teachers are there for a job and not because they are passionate. Simple test which I ask my students to do is recall the names of their teachers and they are hardly able to recall more than one or two, at the most three. Then I ask them what about the rest, they don't seem to remember, and my personal take is it is probably because they didn't leave a mark on your life. Teachers don't earn that much money but what they earn is the gratitude of their students and that is priceless. But understandably in our country our first contact teachers in school are not necessarily driven by passion to teach and most likely are there to make livelihood. As a result of which they fail to ignite the same fire that a passionate person would have. On a more senior level in postgraduation and beyond, particularly in medical sector I have noticed a sense of insecurity in many people and fear that the student will go beyond them. Problem is people who are really passionate about life and things probably in India don't end up being teachers and people who end up being teachers are there for all the reasons other than teaching.

Then who will inspire our children for future. I sincerely believe that both government and private sector should encourage volunteers to teach. Why can't they have volunteer registry and invite them to schools as per their convenience and get them to interact with students. Give them a token of appreciation, like a certificate or momento and I am sure many of us would spare sometime for them and talk to students.

Teaching is a noble profession and I really wish that we restore the nobility associated with it.

This is a quote which a student many years back sent to me with thanks for the help in DAMS – "give a man a fish and you feed him for a day; teach a man to fish and you feed him for a lifetime" and make a difference in my life.

□

## Bird Eye's View to Your Rescue

Sometimes things which are obvious to everybody else; are opaque to the person affected. Common sense is so uncommon at times or probably most of times that we overlook it. When faced with a road block and no win situation, just stand back; look at things from a distance and from an outsider's perspective. Talk to people and they will tell you common sense. Don't ask for advice just talk. Try to see things from a different perspective and they will probably not look as complex as they did. Similar things happen in Radiology, there are times I see junior residents looking at a CXR too closely and missing the obvious finding. All I do is pull them back and ask them to first have a bird eye's view and then focus on pathology. I think same applies to all physicians, look at the problem in broader way and then narrow it down.

When we know the trick for medicine, why not apply in day to day life. Problems or roadblocks can be easily solved when looked at by outsider's perspective, while involved people lose sight.

***Imagine the mountain, will you see it clearly while climbing up or from a distance.***

□

## "What if it's All a Lie?"

There are people who believe everything on their face value about what they hear or read in school or newspapers or television. Do you realize history is written by winners or on directions of the winners; not by independent observers. Think about our entire history book which you mug up assuming everything to be factual, think of them from a different perspective. On my visit to London last year, our British guide was describing the achievements of British with pride and when I told her that we actually think negatively about their era, she was genuinely surprised and wanted to know how our history books describe their era. Now go back little in time, ages before did we actually know how our past was, who was right, and who was shown to be right by paid historians. Think about religion, how are you sure that the translators hadn't added their interpretations to our religious texts. At least now we are living in a unique generation where history is being recorded parallel by authorities and people both on Internet. This is the power of the web today.

□

## Imitation Without Passion

I believe imitation is the highest form of flattery. Some people just get it wrong because we do things which we strongly feel for and some people just copy and paste without the soul behind.

That's why imitation usually fails. Because they copy the idea but they don't have the passion behind.

*You can copy what I do, but you don't have my reasons, you don't have my passion.*

*Remember, even the best imitation in the world is not even half as good as a poor original.*

□

## To Know that "I Don't Know" is the Key

What is even more dangerous than not knowing? All of us have seen and met people who seem to be doing things grossly wrong and are totally oblivious of it. They are actually ignorant of shortcomings. Successful people know where they lack and know when to take the back seat and let the people who know the way take the driver's seat. While the ignorant ones forcefully keep driving and waste significant time and often miss the chance completely.

Here is my two cents to it:

Accept that no one know everything (including you). This is a humble realization, it empties you and allow you to accept knowledge freely.

Write down what you don't know. Once in a while introspect and jot down where you are ignorant and make it a point to fill it up.

Take help as sometimes the 'obvious' may not be evident to the person concerned. And also help others to see 'their gaps' without being intrusive or you will end up losing friends.

*Actually, it is never about what you know. It is always about being aware of the gaps, being aware of what you don't know, which is the key to success.*

*Do You Know What You Don't Know?*

□

## Things You cannot Control

I love conducting seminars for medical students on competitive exams. Very often, I see some or other student will ask about why the government policy is like this, why the exam pattern is like this and they will go on to a confrontation mode.

After letting them speak out their heart, I pause.

I simply remind them, there are always things that you cannot control, you have two months to go for exam and changing the world would take much longer than that and revising your syllabus is by all means a simple and more doable and achievable target.

Haven't we all at some point of time in life devoted all our energy into debating what is wrong in the system, and lost the game to people who were focussed on the system. Haven't we?

*Let's learn to segregate things. Learn to ignore things you cannot control and channelize energy into positive creativity.*

*Change will happen when it is to happen! Not overnight, for ROME wasn't built in a day.*

☐

## Imperfections

He wanted to be perfect. Just as they show in movies. He always wanted to be like the TV advertisements. They all showed glimpses of the perfect people and their perfect world. He structured his own life to be perfect. Everything picture perfect. Rich, famous and plastic.

### Years later

When he was no longer young he didn't look perfect. In his last few days in the hospital, he had his old wife, holding his hand. He looked out of the window; saw few perfect buildings and among them few imperfect trees. There he realised his mistake, nature was beautiful.

*In our attempt to create perfect structures, we create symmetric buildings and irregular, chaotic nature that always appears to be more enchanting. The so-called 'Imperfections' are the way of the nature. Don't try to be perfect, we are the best when we are at comfort zone with our own imperfections.*

□

## Prejudice

*He was a short guy. In school, he saw the playground and loved the way others were playing on the ground. He quickly ran towards the ground. He went to the basketball court. His sport teacher looked at him with a queer smile and said "kid this is not for you". He hadn't even touched the ball yet. This was first time when he actually realized that he was a short guy. But he was adamant and wanted to prove himself. He always imagined himself to be a tall, macho guy. Game started, someone passed the ball to him, as the ball raced to him, and he became conscious of the eyes looking at him. They seemed to mock him, laugh at his height. He became more and more self-conscious. Ball slipped from his hand and people watching the game laughed. It became unbearable.*

*Have you ever wondered our single act of prejudice at times can lead to self-doubt and agony to people concerned. Let's stop generalizing.*

*It is not the stereotypes who always win.*

□

## Aim for Progress not Perfection

A student once complained to me that he is not able to complete the entire syllabus to perfection. Not able to answer 100% of the questions. I was wondering why 'I' never had such a doubt during my preparation. Probably, because I always knew that perfection is not my target. I always aimed for progress and improvement. Idea is to continuously identify your weaknesses and improve them. Medical science is huge and people who claim to be perfect are actually fake. In this field, strive to be a constant learner.

*A perpetual student.*

I still remember a very senior professor telling me that he still learns something new every day. That's the eternal truth. We are all students of medicine and let's enjoy this learning process. We are in a unique position to learn about our own selves and disease.

*Blessed are those who keep learning and know that there is still a lot more to learn.*

□

# Far Away World

In the dream world, there is a far away land where mind is quiet. Where time doesn't matter and moments of joy linger on.

In real life, there is noise just too much of noise. There are questions to answer. Things to do. Goals to achieve.

In between, there is a zone before you wake up when you can perceive the joy of the dreamland and noise of the reality together.

At that moment you know exactly what's missing and then....

*The alarm!*

*Reality returns! and your eyes open up to the new day altogether.*

□

# GRATITUDE

Thank
You

## World Without You

Just for a moment, imagine a world without you. Don't be scared to think.

Now did you actually visualize anything stopping because of your absence?

Now imagine a few days later no one is even talking about you.

Yes, that's the normal human philosophy. We remember the survivors only.

*This exercise would help you gain humility; you are but a tiny insignificant speck in the universe.*

*Use your time wisely. Value people, who care, don't keep grudges, appreciate the fine moments you get and finally keep your priorities right, choose people over things and live your passion to its best before the time runs out.*

*Stop caring about what people think because They don't really care right now and surely, they won't even remember once you are not there.*

□

## Do You Have Some Free 'Space'?

Some people are really full of themselves. *They are centre of the universe for themselves. I, me and myself are their driving words.*

At first look they appear charming with their immense self-obsession appearing like confidence and they attract people and relationships. Slowly, the trouble begins. Being so full about one selves hardly gives space to anyone else and their relationships begin to crumble. These people make poor team players as they want the glory and all the credit to themselves. People keep leaving them and they keep justifying their actions as shortsightedness.

There is a thin line between a self-preserving pride and overflowing with your own self. To learn something new, to build a team or to build a relationship you need some empty space.

Let me leave you with some reality checks to calculate your space quotient.

Do you remember last time you said, I don't know this?

Do you often give credit to others for their good work?

If you see a single glass of water left in the tray and you are thirsty, would you even wait to see if others had their share before gulping it down?

If confronted with a fact that belief you held for so long is entirely wrong, would you accept it?

Create some space for others' perspective to fit in and you will evolve in no time. You retain the positive exuberance of youth because you are willing to learn and accommodate.

Remain full of yourselves and you would evolve as a cynical critic.

*Realization that you are nothing but a tiny speck in the grand scale of things, humbles you and empties you and allows you to accept new knowledge and opinions.*

*Do you have some 'free' space?*

□

## Sense of Entitlement

Scene 1: He was driving down the mad rush. It was very crowded. Life in general as always was very busy. He was honking nonstop. All of a sudden an autorickshaw hit the side of his fancy car. He lost his cool and came out and abused. He caught hold of the driver and hit him hard. He was entitled to drive on road, how could someone dare to block his way.

Scene 2: She was standing in queue in the airline and announcement was made stating that flight was delayed. She snapped. How could they do it.... She started abusing the ground staff as if it was in their control.

Scene 3: He went for a job interview, he knew all about the pay scale he was entitled to. He knew about his skill and knowledge, so he didn't say much. He has a degree and he is entitled to a particular salary scale.

*Today is the era of the entitlement, people strongly believe that they are entitled to the services and benefits; they are brash about it. Everyone seems to know their entitlements but none of them is aware as to what they are supposed to do.*

*May be we are overcrowded.*

*But gone is the generation of gratitude and humility, we have become an era of the entitlement.*

□

## Circle of Good

There are times when you feel hopeless about the world. Hopeless about everything. Nothing and nobody seems to be right. All appear self-centred and fake.

But every now and then you meet someone who helps your cause selflessly. Without much expectation in return; someone helps you or goes out of the way for you. That is where you know the reason why we survive on this planet, despite everything being so wrong.

We survive because of a few good men.

When you realize this you tend to pay back your saviour by helping someone else selflessly. You carry forward the unsaid principle of faith and help someone else, with whom you have no self-interest.

*That's the circle of good, which keeps the world going.*

□

## Be Humble, Be Yourself

Most fundamental trait which marks a good learner is his humility. Learning is a lifelong process. Day you stop being humble enough to receive, that day your influx of wisdom and knowledge slows down. Probably, this is the reason in ancient times, Indian *gurukuls* made even princes beg for alms to learn humility. If you are too full of yourself, there is no space for new knowledge or wisdom to enter. Sometimes, I feel we were born humble, we acquire pride on the way, but life in itself manages to give you a lesson in humility. As C.S. Lewis said, "Humility is not thinking less of yourself, it's thinking of yourself less."

□

# Gratitude

Easiest way to rise in life is to have gratitude. Gratitude somehow has been underrated in successful people's life stories. I believe when you express it routinely, you achieve true success.

Be grateful. For every tiny thing people do for you, be grateful for all the small blessings in life. Don't assume you are born to receive all. Remember to say thank you for what you get and life will shower more blessings on you.

Make sure you appreciate a kind gesture, make sure you are thankful to your subordinates, colleagues, friends and family for support they give you all the time. Be grateful, stay grounded and humble, and let the success do the talking. Don't look at life as a glass half empty, see it as the half full glass and bring positivity in life of everyone associated with you.

Once you become oriented toward looking for things to be grateful for, you will find that you begin to appreciate simple pleasures and things that you previously took for granted. Gratitude should not be just a reaction to getting what you want, but an all-the-time gratitude, the kind where you notice the little things and where you constantly look for the good even in unpleasant situations. Today, start bringing gratitude to your experiences, instead of waiting for a positive experience in order to feel grateful; in this way, you'll be on your way toward becoming a master of gratitude.

Amen!

□

# CREATIVITY

# The Coffee House

There he was. Always on the corner seat at the coffee house facing the road. He sat on the same seat every day. He seemed to look at the people passing by with blank eyes looking at a faraway in the infinity. In between he would sip at his black coffee and would type intently on his laptop. He had a story to tell.

Faceless people passing by never really saw him but found way into his stories. He looked at them and tried to imagine the story behind each of them.

What was the young woman round the corner doing? Restlessly looking at her phone, may be her husband was delayed somewhere and she was desperately waiting to hear from him.

There was a group of young boys in the coffee house, shouting and laughing. What was that about? Yesterday's cricket match. They were ignorant about troubles of life and they were least bothered with what was going around.

Meanwhile, the cafe waitress would smile at him and ask him if he wanted some more coffee, he looked into her eyes, trying to gauge if she also had a story to tell.

There was hustle bustle all around. But all he could make out was a familiar hum that all of us do.

Place was alive and full of stories.

He somehow knew why writers in the past would sit along the roadside bars and look for inspiration.

That is why he was here. To write

*To bring it out of him. To bring the best out of him. He wanted to write about 'real' people with 'real' stories. One that would set him free.*

*That coffee house was his inspiration. His place of solitude.*

□

## Ideas are Parasites

*Inception: Cobb: What is the most resilient parasite? Bacteria? A virus? An intestinal worm? An idea. Resilient...highly contagious. Once an idea has taken hold of the brain it's almost impossible to eradicate. An idea that is fully formed – fully understood – that sticks; right in there somewhere.*

*Read this quote in the morning and I am unable to get it off my mind. This is my problem as well, when I get an idea, it does not let me go to sleep, my desire to implement it gets me restless. That's probably the way of nature as well and that's the beginning of creativity.*

□

## Will Crowd Sourcing One Day Solve the Mystery of Life?

Time is the key: We just don't have time there is too much to do and too little time we have. We don't have gratifying answers to all the questions of life. I am sure we are yet to find the true details of the past and the future. Leave alone the past or future many questions of 'present' are yet to be answered. There are so many things I want to work on, so many places I want to see, so many books I want to read and time just seems to fly. Then I think of great thinkers and scientists like Einstein who came close to answering the 'questions' but still time remained the big constraint as ever. I feel answer to all the queries of today will come from convergence of science, religion and ancient knowledge. More I travel, more this belief becomes stronger. Collective work and crowd sourcing is the way forward where thinkers and philosophers can work together on a virtual platform to answer the questions. One human life is just too less of time....

☐

## 'I am Bored' Leads to Creativity

This is what I have learnt about myself. I was not the creative kinds in school, trust me I was the studious kinds desperate to win, to become a doctor, and was preoccupied with Test Preparation. Similar thing happened in college with pressure of being a post-graduate in good subject. I became creative when I got time and when I was not hard pressed for goals and had time for myself. Going back in time, I am forced to think whenever I got bored of doing what I was doing; I found my creative side to do something interesting. Same instinct I noticed in my two and half year old son, whatever toys you may get for him, he will get bored and find his own source of entertainment. So here is what I would like to recommend to entire schooling processes, that ***"Let them get bored of routine and they will create the new and exciting future."*** For maybe we all are forcing our kids too compete, that they don't get time to express their creativity and innovative skills which now has proved to be much more valuable in today's world.

□

## Circle of Thought

*There she was, sitting on a wheel chair, a very old woman, white hair with wrinkled face and blank eyes. Waiting to board the flight.*

There were younger people around, some posing for pictures, some excited about the next project, group of students going to school picnic full of excitement and energy.

Yet her eyes would remain blank. May be she was thinking about the transience of everything that everybody else seems so excited about.

She was not sad but didn't seem to be happy either.

May be she was thinking of her family, may be about old friends or may be nothing. People passed by, moved around, they didn't seem to notice her.

*Yet, her eyes remained blank.*

□

# Wheels and Wings (Fiction)

**Prehistoric times:** Men wanted to travel to far-off places. They wanted to do things faster. They wanted to create pottery. They wanted to move heavy material from one place to another. This is when they actually invented the wheel. One discovery which changed it all. Life became faster. More and more new places became approachable.

*But what if one wise man hadn't thought about the wheel?*

**Back to today:** No one has so far thought about the concept of the wheel. People don't travel to far-off places. Only few from a tribe venture to far-off places, and seldom come back. Life is moving at a slower pace. Everybody now days are working close to home. People tend to spend more time with each other. You know most people around you. You spend most of your time with friends and family. You rarely meet people outside your proximity zone. Life seems to be bit longer than usual.

There are some mutants who actually have developed rudimentary wings on their backs. They can fly for short distances. They are half men, half birds. Desire to travel is so strong, that natural selection seems to have favoured these mutants. Remember there are no wheels in this world.

*People want to take out more out of their time in life, they want to run faster and faster, who knows, had it not been for the wheel, we may have developed wings by now....*

□

# ENTREPRENEURSHIP

## The Test of 'Time'

As a kid I always used to wonder why organizations and stores across the world write on their boards, tag lines like 'Since 1831', 'since 1920', etc. But after running my own organizations, both DAMS and TeleRad Providers I have realized that we have actually improved, and added processes every year. We are not the same organization anymore; we have changed and evolved with time keeping up to date with technologies and consumer needs. Now I have understood the value of organizations which have survived more than 100 years with changing customer base and mindset, have actually stood the test of time. This shows their patience and willingness to change according to times. It tells us about adaptability or else their products would have stopped making sense. Time is the most important test for any organization, because it does not forgive, if you don't respect changing times you will perish in no time. Many people/start ups give up in initial years. There is chasm between starting something new and becoming mainstream. People who become successful are the ones who cross the chasm by surviving the test of time. Organizations are like people, they age, with age some mature into adaptable system while some become senile, lose connect with the consumer base and perish away. True relationships and great organisations stand the test of time.

*May we get the gift to come up with ideas that will last. Ideas that will stand the 'test of time'.*

□

## Organized Chaos

Many people try there level best to make processes and workflow, free from chaos hoping for a perfect organization with everything in place. Most start ups feel that larger corporations are fully organized. But what I have learnt in fact is that there is always a chaos in every organization, to achieve a goal but the only ones who are able to direct it towards a common goal, are able to do well. Hence, my term for successful people and great organizations is organized chaos. At the 'micro' level, you will observe chaos but at a 'macro' level you will find the 'organized chaos' moving forward, inching upwards. Something happens in exams, sometimes things actually appear chaotic but as long as the entire process is moving towards a common goal, it is alright.

*Probably secret to success is to not creating a picture perfect scenario (which is usually far from realistic) rather 'the secret' is organizing your chaos towards a common goal, so the larger picture makes sense even when the individual components are chaotic.*

□

# King Midas and the Story of Entrepreneurship

People go for 'Gold', we tend to idolize people who had the touch of MIDAS (who when touched anything turned into gold after being granted a wish by a fairy) But as the legend goes, when King Midas touched food and his daughter – they turned into gold too. That is when he understood that his gift was a bane and so was his loath for gold, and ended up cursing his greed. I believe this fable, holds a deeper meaning in today's world where 'WE' chase money and then end up turning food into gold and finally end up starving. If we don't leave the greed for gold, the relationships we touch we will lose them too. Idea in life is to chase dreams, chase passion, touch lives,and make a difference rather than to materialize anything and everything into gold.

*Midas Touch as I would say is surely a gift but when your desire for gold spills into personal life, there things start going wrong for entrepreneurs.*

□

# Find Your True Passion

Till the time we are chasing something which may be either a new project, new gadget, new car or even a new accessory, it becomes interesting, it becomes the focus of our attention, and we find pleasure in trying to get it and once we get it its just happiness that flows around. But soon the happiness fades away and as the child gets bored the 'trophy' no longer appeals to him as much as it once did and we move onto the next chase. On the other hand, lets talk about what you are passionate about for when you chase your true passion, the intensity and joy do not fade, the desire to chase and to win just keeps growing stronger and stronger and that is when 'true' success emerges....

Remember "The most powerful weapon on earth is the human soul on fire." As rightly said by *Sir Ferdinand Foch*.

□

## People Never Forget How You Made Them Feel

Just wondering why Facebook has become integral part of our lives. Probably, the answer lies in the fact that our memory about people and places works just similar to Facebook. Try recalling a place or a person and you will notice that actually you don't recall a "video" it is usually a series of still photos, few sentences and the way you felt with that person that comes to your mind. Our entire perception of the world is a blurred recall biased by the way we felt at one particular time. Somehow, Facebook helps in striking the right emotional string in aiding that recall some close relations, some acquaintances, few pictures, few emotions and few stories. Everyone of us has a story to tell pictures to share, and emotions to share with people who see the world from the window created by the ones who have the story to tell.

That is life that is what it is, sum total of your memories and feelings attached together. For it is rightly said people will forget, what you said, people will forget what you did, but people will never forget how you made them feel.

□

# Touching Lives

Who are the ones who are content with their work? Who are the ones who are truly successful? Is it that name, money or fame for that matter matters?

To me, true success is one which can be measured in terms of number of lives that have been touched and differences made. More lives you touch, more meaningful difference you make in their lives, and more successful you are. That is what is the difference between material success and success in its real sense. Let us all strive to be humble, grounded, and feel for lives that we touch along our path. Let us do our best, as physicians where we have the unique opportunity to touch other lives, as teachers where we can make difference in lives of our students, in our work where we touch the lives of customers and colleagues and above all in family.

In the end, what really matters is lives touched and meaningful difference made down the path, interestingly most of the times you will not even know the difference you make in his or her life. As organisations and as entrepreneurs we touch the lives of our clients and employees both. Positive leadership lies in making a meaningful difference and success is always the number of people touched. Let's hope that we stay strong and humble enough and continue to make difference in people's lives.

Amen!

□

## Gambler's Spirit

There resides a 'SPIRIT' of a gambler inside everyone who is successful. Planners and people who take too long to calculate seldom make it large. You cannot know it all before playing, so there is always an element of gambling, stakes that you put in are not in safe limits always. Sometimes you just have to put in all you have for the sake of winning, and risks are just as real as gambling, but the joy of winning is seductive. The thrill of unpredictability and the joy of winning are unmatched. Lure to continue betting is also quiet addictive. And I am not talking of gambling as in playing cards or casinos; I am talking of gambling that we do every day in our lives,work,and dealings and that is what makes life so exciting. To me the true gambler's desire is to win it all and still even if you lose, it doesn't matter. For they say, "greatest risk is in not taking any risks."

□

## Gambler's Spirit

There resides a 'SPIRIT' of a gambler inside everyone who is successful. Planners and people who take too long to calculate seldom make it large. You cannot know it all before playing, so there is always an element of gambling, stakes that you put in are not in safe limits always. Sometimes you just have to put in all you have for the sake of winning, and risks are just as real as gambling, but the joy of winning is seductive. The thrill of unpredictability and the joy of winning are unmatched. Lure to continue betting is also quiet addictive. And I am not talking of gambling as in playing cards or casinos; I am talking of gambling that we do every day in our lives,work,and dealings and that is what makes life so exciting. To me the true gambler's desire is to win it all and still even if you lose, it doesn't matter. For they say, "greatest risk is in not taking any risks."

□



## Find Your True Passion

Till the time we are chasing something which may be either a new project, new gadget, new car or even a new accessory, it becomes interesting, it becomes the focus of our attention, and we find pleasure in trying to get it and once we get it its just happiness that flows around. But soon the happiness fades away and as the child gets bored the 'trophy' no longer appeals to him as much as it once did and we move onto the next chase. On the other hand, lets talk about what you are passionate about for when you chase your true passion, the intensity and joy do not fade, the desire to chase and to win just keeps growing stronger and stronger and that is when 'true' success emerges....

Remember "The most powerful weapon on earth is the human soul on fire." As rightly said by *Sir Ferdinand Foch.*

□

# People Never Forget How You Made Them Feel

Just wondering why Facebook has become integral part of our lives. Probably, the answer lies in the fact that our memory about people and places works just similar to Facebook. Try recalling a place or a person and you will notice that actually you don't recall a "video" it is usually a series of still photos, few sentences and the way you felt with that person that comes to your mind. Our entire perception of the world is a blurred recall biased by the way we felt at one particular time. Somehow, Facebook helps in striking the right emotional string in aiding that recall some close relations, some acquaintances, few pictures, few emotions and few stories. Everyone of us has a story to tell pictures to share, and emotions to share with people who see the world from the window created by the ones who have the story to tell.

That is life that is what it is, sum total of your memories and feelings attached together. For it is rightly said people will forget, what you said, people will forget what you did, but people will never forget how you made them feel.

□



# Touching Lives

Who are the ones who are content with their
Who are the ones who are truly successful? Is i
name, money or fame for that matter matters?

To me, true success is one which can be mea
in terms of number of lives that have been touche
differences made. More lives you touch, more mean
difference you make in their lives, and more succ
you are. That is what is the difference between m
success and success in its real sense. Let us all striv
humble, grounded, and feel for lives that we touch
our path. Let us do our best, as physicians where w
the unique opportunity to touch other lives, as te
where we can make difference in lives of our stu
in our work where we touch the lives of custome
colleagues and above all in family.

In the end, what really matters is lives touch
meaningful difference made down the path, intere
most of the times you will not even know the diff
you make in his or her life. As organisations
entrepreneurs we touch the lives of our clien
employees both. Positive leadership lies in ma
meaningful difference and success is always the n
of people touched. Let's hope that we stay stro
humble enough and continue to make differe
people's lives.

Amen!

## Leap of Faith

What kind of person are you? Are you a typical cynical person who believes everything is wrong, everyone is corrupt? Or you are the one who 'TRUSTS'. And who do you think is more likely to succeed, the cynic or the one with faith. You will be surprised to know more successful people are the ones those who trust others. One example which I often quote to people is about small time business operators in India: most people in India work like 'water-selling boy' whose job is to sell water bottles to people in the bus, bus starts moving; the boy doesn't leave the bottle as he is not sure if he will get the money or not and man doesn't leave the ten rupee note as he is afraid that he might lose his hard earned money, while truly speaking risk of transaction not happening could have been very very less had one of them 'TRUSTED' the person on other side and would have culminated into a useful one for either of the two. Everybody will tell you to hold on, not to trust, while people who have faith in others are the ones who are actually taking chances and are the ones who are building teams. In other words, successful people are more likely to take the leap of faith, and get the things going, as compared to cynics who tend to stop progress from happening and finally lack behind. May be it involves a subconscious element of your brain in making a judgement so as to when to take the leap, but somehow deep down there in your heart you and only you know the truth and if you feel it is right, take the leap. Be it work, relationship, employment, hiring, or starting new ventures for that matter – my mantra is simple – understand, trust your instincts and if the feeling is right take the leap.

□

# Nokia Story: World is Changing Faster than You can Imagine

My first mobile like almost everyone here, was a 'Nokia' and when we are part of the generation who can actually feel the changing world, when Nokia announced being acquired by Microsoft, Nokia CEO ended his speech by saying "we didn't do anything wrong, but somehow, we lost". Upon saying that, all his management team, himself included, teared sadly.

*They didn't do anything wrong, however, the world changed too fast.*

On a side note, this was probably a new beginning for Microsoft. And recently I had brought Microsoft Surface Pro4 (my first non-Apple tab) and hadn't taken my laptop out of the cupboard ever since then. Yet another change seems to be coming on mobile and tablet platform with Microsoft going the aggressive way. I feel they would populate the windows based ecosystem to compete with android and apple, and lead yet another change.

World is changing faster than anyone can imagine. Traditional way of doing things is changing faster than ever before. We are living in a hyper-linked and feedback governed world. Movie is going to be released today and by evening your facebook wall is going to be full of reviews and by next morning verdict will be announced at the same place 'THE WALL'. Even before going on a vacation, you need to know what to expect from trip advisor. You need to learn to run even before you know how to walk.

*There is nothing permanent except change.*

□

## Doctors and Entrepreneurship

Traditionally, doctors are not considered entrepreneurs in its true sense and usually medicine is considered 'round the clock' work and hardly gives you time for anything else. Several factors contribute to this perception. To start with the usual impression of a medico in society in general is someone who is risk averse and deals with facts rather than imagination. While as an entrepreneur you need to have that rebellious, risk taking instinct along with an ability to foresee, the so-called vision.

All this while healthcare was filled with gaps in delivery and challenges, while so-called traditional managers and investors are usually naive to the deep healthcare problems. This has lead to immense change in the doctor's mindset over last few years. More and more doctors can be seen rising to the opportunity and are utilizing their innate skills of medicine and capability to work under stress. Rise of the doctor-enterpreneur is inevitable as 'WE' see gaps in the system which need to be addressed by someone who is into it who is deep into the system and is aware from "root to the top". Rise in IT sector specially e-commerce and virtual reality now attracts young doctors to look for parallel models in healthcare. Scope of tele-medicine, role of wearables, electronic health records, social networks, tele-education, e-prescriptions, practice management; list of IT applications being tried in healthcare appears endless.

Entrepreneurship is not always for profit, there is something called as "Social Entrepreneurship" which helps to channelize capital and energy in research for new treatments. Entrepreneurship-based model for medical research which focuses on outcomes which will make maximum impact in treatment modalities available can lead to outcomes that are beyond imagination at present.

I sincerely and firmly believe that healthcare will benefit from the apparent 'misfits' while classically we tend to ask the doctors to confirm for uniformity in protocols. These "misfits with entrepreneur like mindset" if given a proper platform will bring the much desired breakthrough and will change the way things are being done.

*Doctors cannot continue to lose ownership of the next era of healthcare to IT geeks and investing geniuses. Next decade will see rise of more docpreneurs as I would like to say, and will bring unique blend of entrepreneur like risk taking abilities and insights of the healthcare problem from inside.*

□□□